D0913763

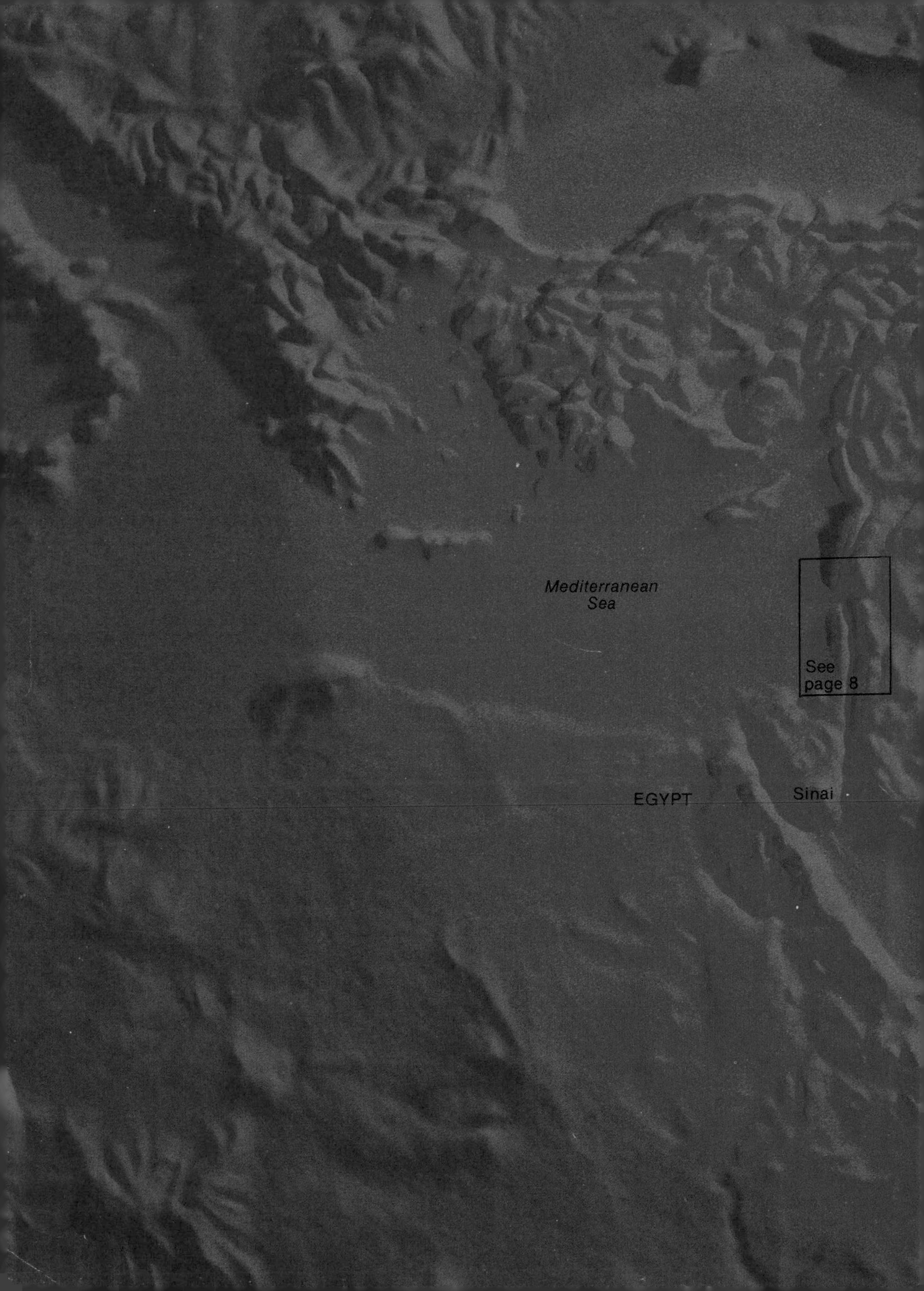

*Mediterranean
Sea*

EGYPT   Sinai

See
page 8

Setting
of Eden

Ur

Red Sea

Copyright © 1972 and 1973 Lion Publishing

Photographs and notes by David Alexander
Revised and expanded by Robin Keeley

Published by
Lion Publishing plc
Icknield Way, Tring, Herts, England
ISBN 0 85648 563 2
ISBN 0 85648 701 5 (Israeli edition)
Albatross Books
PO Box 320, Sutherland, NSW 2232, Australia
ISBN 0 86760 462 X

First edition in two volumes:
Photo-Guide to the New Testament 1972
Photo-Guide to the Old Testament 1973

New one-volume edition 1981
Reprinted 1982
This paperback edition 1983

Scripture text, *The Holy Bible, New International Version:*
Copyright © New York International Bible Society, 1978

Typeset by V & M Graphics Ltd, Aylesbury, Bucks
Printed and bound in Great Britain
by Purnell and Sons Ltd, Paulton, Bristol

The Lion
Photoguide
to the Bible

Contents

Part One: The Old Testament

Part Two: The New Testament

Tyre

LEBANON

Hazor

GALILEE

Mount Carmel △

△ Mount Tabor

△ Hill of Moreh

Megiddo ● ● Jezreel

△ Mount Gilboa

Shechem

SAMARIA

Mountains of
Samaria ● Shiloh

River Jordan

Gezer ● ● Jericho

Gibeon

Kiriath-Jearim ● **Jerusalem**

Bethlehem ●

Judean
Mountains

Lachish ● ● Hebron

● Ein Gedi

King's Highway

● Massada

Negev Desert

● Massada

EDOM

Avdat

Part One

The Old Testament

Introduction

It is a rewarding experience to be able to visit the Middle East, and see for oneself the places where the events of the Bible took place. But many of the Old Testament sites are not on the main tourist routes – and in any case not many will have the good fortune to be able to make such a trip at all.

This book will help fill the need. The pictures recapture the way of life and events so graphically described in the Old Testament. They open a window on the history, literature and environment of Bible times. They show the relevance of some of the archaeological discoveries made over the last century which bring us face to face with the ancient civilizations flourishing in Bible times.

The Old Testament spans the ages, from the beginning of time to the dark days after the fall of Jerusalem, the exile of God's people to Babylon and their return. The narrative ranges from history to poetry, from law to prophecy. Written over more than a thousand years, it both reflects the age in which it was written and carries a power which makes it relevant to all time.

The fact that the Old Testament so often reflects contemporary life means that our understanding of it can be helped as we see it against its background. The life of the desert tent-dwellers enables us to picture Abraham and the patriarchs. The cracked, sun-bleached salt rocks near the Dead Sea evoke the catastrophe which overwhelmed Sodom and Gomorrah. The mountains of Sinai and barren wastes of the Negev desert vividly reflect the setting of the wanderings in the wilderness and giving of the law.

Some of the sites have an interest which is more directly historical. Today there may be no more than a litter of ruins and fallen stones: but these are the actual remains of Shiloh or Shechem, Lachish or Gezer. Some of the archaeological sites are easier to imagine as they appeared in Bible times: Jericho, or Megiddo, with its Canaanite 'high place' and buildings from the time of Solomon, or Hazor with its gateway and pillars – and even a wall hastily built because of impending invasion. The Old Testament is not a collection of myths. It was about real people living in real places whose remains can still be seen today. The narrative has, in fact, at many places been shown to be reliable and relevant by modern discoveries. The historical accuracy of the Bible has been rediscovered too by many who read it in the light of contemporary research.

A shepherd leading his flock, gazelles on the mountains, wool being dyed scarlet, water in the desert, the cedars of Lebanon . . . much of the familiar language of the Old Testament lives afresh when it is pictured in this way. Today it is only in traditional areas that one can still see the wooden plough, the camel market, the flocks round a well, so it is good that as city life and mechanization increase the traditional setting of biblical life can be recorded and appreciated while it is still possible.

The main aim of this book is to encourage the reader to turn again to the whole Bible for himself. There he will see God in action with real people in actual situations. God who called out a people to live in faith in himself, who delivered them from slavery and showed them the way to live, is the same God as the God and Father of Jesus Christ, who showed the way to newness of life and won man's freedom by his death and resurrection. It is this faith, the theme of this book, which is so vital and relevant today.

Donald J. Wiseman
Professor of Assyriology in the University of London

Ancient Israel extended 'from Dan to Beersheba'. Near Dan in the extreme north is the source of the River Jordan. Its springs come out from the limestone foothills of Mount Hermon. The water is forced through the stones with an energy and power that make it immediately a rushing stream.

1
FATHERS OF A NATION

Creation

'In the beginning God created the heavens and the earth . . .' Genesis 1:1

The first chapter of Genesis proclaims God as source and maker of all things. The teeming universe sprang from his command with all the energy and life of a mountain stream. The creation is presented as a drama in six acts, and at the end of each comes the refrain: 'And God saw that it was good.' God's creativity culminated in the creation of man, made in his 'image and likeness'. And on the seventh day God rested.

Eden

'The Lord God formed man from the dust of the ground and breathed into his nostrils the breath of life, and man became a living being. Now the Lord God had planted a garden in the east, in Eden; and there he put the man he had formed. And the Lord God made all kinds of trees grow out of the ground – trees that were pleasing to the eye and good for food. In the middle of the garden were the tree of life and the tree of the knowledge of good and evil.' Genesis 2:7–9

The picture was taken further down the Jordan River, as it flows down below sea level, south of the Lake of Galilee. Eden itself was given a setting 'in the east', the rivers watering it evoking the richness of the Mesopotamian basin before man made it a desert.

The story of the garden of Eden is of man making a choice – to go the way of independence from God rather than dependence on him. It pictures the struggle humanity has made throughout the generations to find fulfilment on our own terms, without acknowledging God's sovereignty. In Adam, we disobeyed God's command. It was seen as a restriction – we wanted freedom. But in doing so we lost the freedom to be the people God made us to be. Inevitably, fellowship with God was broken. Cut off from God, the source of life and harmony, man and all creation was turned from good to evil. The twist that seems to distort the goodness of nature, and the fatal flaw of sin at the heart of human character, both stem from this tragic 'fall'. The Bible shows sin affecting humanity right from our earliest origins and infecting us ever since.

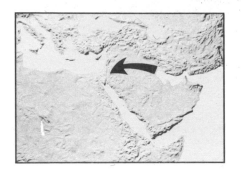

The call of Abraham

'The Lord had said to Abram, "Leave your country, your people and your father's household and go to the land I will show you. I will make you into a great nation and I will bless you; I will make your name great, and you will be a blessing . . . and all peoples on earth will be blessed through you." . . . He took his wife Sarai, his nephew Lot, all the possessions they had accumulated and the people they had acquired in Haran, and they set out for the land of Canaan . . .' Genesis 12:1-5

After all the failures described in Genesis 4–11, God's way of making a new start was by calling one man. Abraham's obedience to God's call was the beginning of the story of salvation for the world. From him came not only the 'great nation' God promised, but also, through his descendant Jesus, a community of faith that has brought blessing to 'all peoples on earth'.

Abraham left the heart of the civilized world of his time to live the life of a nomad. Ur of the Chaldees was a highly developed city of many buildings and considerable sophistication, on the River Euphrates in what is now southern Iraq. Abraham's response to God's call took him first of all to Haran in modern Syria, where his father Terah died. But then the call was repeated, and Abraham moved south through Canaan, the 'land of promise' that is central to the Old Testament story.

The bedouin sheikh pictured here shows how the desert 'dwellers in tents' have lived for centuries. Using goats' skins in winter and sackcloth in the heat of summer, their tents are spread with carpets. The men recline on cushions round the earth fire-place. A more settled way of life would not enable them to find the best grazing for their livestock, their means of livelihood. So closely interdependent were animals and men in the nomad encampment that it was said of Abraham, 'he had sheep, oxen, he-asses, menservants, maidservants, she-asses, and camels.'

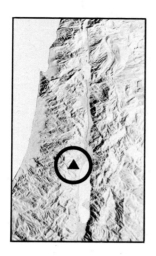

Abraham and Lot

'Abram said to Lot, "Let's not have any quarrelling between you and me, or between your herdsmen and mine, for we are brothers. Is not the whole land before you? Let's part company. If you go to the left, I'll go to the right; if you go to the right, I'll go to the left." Lot looked up and saw that the whole plain of the Jordan was well watered, like the garden of the Lord . . . So Lot chose for himself the whole plain of the Jordan and set out towards the east. The two men parted company: Abram lived in the land of Canaan, while Lot lived among the cities of the plain and pitched his tents near Sodom. Now the men of Sodom were wicked and were sinning greatly against the Lord . . .' Genesis 13:8–13

Famine had driven Abraham and his family to Egypt, where he behaved in a cowardly way and earned Pharaoh's contempt. On his return to Canaan, he was rich in flocks and herds and tents. But it had been a long, weary trek up through the Negev desert, and the herdsmen were quarrelling bitterly. The nobility with which Abraham acted in this situation suggests that he learnt well from his Egyptian failure. It says a lot for his attitude that he offered his nephew first choice of territory.

Lot's decision was based entirely on practical considerations – he went where the grazing looked best. But in choosing that way he ignored the call of God which had brought them there in the first place. And his choice proved to have other implications. The rich cities of the plain were in a state of moral decadence, and Lot moved his tent from a land under promise into a land under judgement.

The choice Abraham offered Lot as they looked north was between the fertile pastures of the rift valley and the poorer grazing of the Judean hills. Lot chose to take his herds to the east, so putting himself outside the boundaries of the land where God's blessing was promised.

Hebron

'The Lord said to Abram after Lot had parted from him, "Lift up your eyes from where you are and look north and south, east and west. All the land that you see I will give to you and your offspring for ever. I will make your offspring like the dust of the earth, so that if anyone could count the dust, then your offspring could be counted. Go, walk through the length and breadth of the land, for I am giving it to you." So Abram moved his tents and went to live near the great trees of Mamre at Hebron, where he built an altar to the Lord.' Genesis 13:14–18

When Lot moved down into the valley, Abraham settled his household at Mamre, a mile or two south of Hebron. It is hard to imagine the sense of destiny he must have felt as he obeyed the command, 'walk through the land . . . I am giving it to you.'

When his wife Sarah died, Abraham took the opportunity to establish a more secure foothold in the land by buying a plot of ground with a cave, as a family burial-ground. Isaac and Rebekah, Leah and Jacob were all later buried there. The long and intricate account in Genesis 23 of his purchase of the plot from the Hittites of Canaan shows the importance attached to owning some actual land, bought with money rather than received as a gift: it symbolized Abraham's determination to inhabit this region as a long-term settler, not a temporary nomad.

The Hittites from whom he bought the land were not identical with the race who set up a great civilization in Syria and southern Anatolia around that time, though they may have been remote kindred to them. They were a sub-group of the Canaanites, and the incident indicates the relationship of friendship and tolerance Abraham had earned with them.

Hebron stands at a height of 3,043ft/927m in the mountains south of Jerusalem. The Arabic name for Abraham is al-Khalil er-Rahman, the Friend of the Lord, hence the Arabic name for Hebron – Khalil. The burial-place of Abraham and Sarah, the Cave of Machpelah, is now a shrine. The building over it, pictured here, goes back to the time of Herod, with additions in Byzantine and Crusader times.

The name then given to the Jerusalem hills was the 'mountains of Moriah' so that the place where Abraham built his altar was also to be the site of Solomon's temple (2 Chronicles 3:1). The rocky top of the temple hill is enshrined in the Mosque of Omar which stands there now.

Mount Moriah

'Some time later God tested Abraham. He said to him, "Abraham!" "Here I am," he replied. Then God said, "Take your son, your only son Isaac, whom you love, and go to the region of Moriah. Sacrifice him there as a burnt offering on one of the mountains I will tell you about." Early the next morning Abraham got up and saddled his donkey. He took with him two of his servants and his son Isaac. When he had cut enough wood for the burnt offering, he set out for the place God had told him about. On the third day Abraham looked up and saw the place in the distance. He said to his servants, "Stay here with the donkey while I and the boy go over there. We will worship and then we will come back to you."'
Genesis 22:1–5

At Mamre God had told Sarah she would have a child – and she had laughed in sheer disbelief, for she was past the age for child-bearing. Yet God had promised that Abraham's descendants would be like the stars in number, and like the sand on the sea-shore. The child Isaac was God's fulfilment of his own promise. So when God then seemed to be calling Abraham to the mountains of Moriah to sacrifice his son, the realization of God's own promise, it was a supreme test of Abraham's trust in God's promises as well as his natural love for his son. Abraham's faith was vindicated: a ram caught in a thicket was provided for the sacrifice instead of Isaac.

It is easy to understand how Abraham could have come to believe God was calling him to make this sacrifice – a kind the Old Testament later came to see as 'altogether abominable'. The surrounding tribes regularly offered up their first sons to their idols, to declare the depth of their commitment. Could Abraham's devotion not match theirs? But the unfolding of God's ways soon revealed that the obedience he required was never to be associated with cruelty. He demanded an even more total consecration, but one that always centred on love.

The Dead Sea, or Salt Sea, lies at the deepest point in the long rift valley down which flows the River Jordan. As the heat of the sun evaporates the water, the concentrates of potash and other chemicals build up to amount to 25 per cent of the water content.

The Dead Sea

'The two men said to Lot, "Do you have anyone else here, sons-in-law, sons or daughters, or anyone else in the city who belongs to you? Get them out of here, because we are going to destroy this place. The outcry to the Lord against its people is so great that he has sent us to destroy it."'
Genesis 19:12, 13

The cities of Sodom and Gomorrah are thought to have been in the area of the Dead Sea. Certainly the acrid reek in the air and the rocks bare of vegetation evoke the volcanic catastrophe which overwhelmed them. The perversion and cruelty of the society that emerges from the story of Lot has made them a by-word for corruption ever since. The Lord's judgement was swift and absolute.

Pillars of salt

'Then the Lord rained down burning sulphur on Sodom and Gomorrah – from the Lord out of the heavens. Thus he overthrew those cities and the entire plain, including all those living in the cities – and also the vegetation in the land. But Lot's wife looked back and she became a pillar of salt.'
Genesis 19:24–26

Lot and his daughters escaped alive only because of Abraham's moving and persistent prayer to God (see Genesis 18:16–33). They had to get away immediately and without pausing to regret. Lot's wife hankered for the old life and was overtaken by the burning volcanic ash – just like the victims of Vesuvius at Pompeii. The salt pillars in the picture bear silent witness to God's judgement, but also to his mercy in answering Abraham's prayer.

These great pillars of salt are at the south end of the Dead Sea.

A wife for Isaac

'Then the servant took ten of his master's camels and left, taking with him all kinds of good things from his master. He set out for Aram Naharaim and made his way to the town of Nahor. He made the camels kneel down near the well, outside the town; it was towards evening, the time the women go out to draw water. Then he prayed, "O Lord, God of my master Abraham, give me success today, and show kindness to my master Abraham. See, I am standing beside this spring, and the daughters of the townspeople are coming out to draw water. May it be that when I say to a girl, 'Please let down your jar that I may have a drink,' and she says, 'Drink, and I'll water your camels too' – let her be the one you have chosen for your servant Isaac. By this I will know that you have shown kindness to my master." Before he had finished praying, Rebekah came out with her jar on her shoulder . . .' Genesis 24:10–15

As Abraham neared the end of his life, he had a natural fear that his son Isaac would be drawn away from Canaan, 'the land of promise'. The most likely cause would be the need to find a wife from among their kinsfolk, who had only completed the first stage of the journey, from Chaldea to Syria. And so Abraham sends his chief steward to forestall this danger, and bring a wife back from Haran to Canaan.

Such a mission was highly unlikely to succeed, but the story describes a beautiful instance of spiritual guidance. The steward's prayer was answered: Rebekah was the daughter of Abraham's nephew, and, as it turned out, a wife whom Isaac truly loved.

Abraham's servant retraced the steps of his master's original journey, to Haran in north-west Mesopotamia. The town of Haran had been renamed Nahor. Haran and Nahor were both Abraham's brothers.

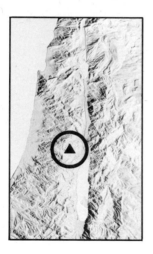

Bethel

'Jacob left Beersheba and set out for Haran. When he reached a certain place, he stopped for the night because the sun had set. Taking one of the stones there, he put it under his head and lay down to sleep. He had a dream in which he saw a stairway resting on the earth, with its top reaching to heaven, and the angels of God were ascending and descending on it. There above it stood the Lord, and he said: "I am the Lord, the God of your father Abraham and the God of Isaac. I will give you and your descendants the land on which you are lying. Your descendants will be like the dust of the earth . . . " When Jacob awoke from his sleep, he thought, "Surely the Lord is in this place, and I was not aware of it." He was afraid and said, "How awesome is this place! This is none other than the house of God; this is the gate of heaven." Early the next morning Jacob took the stone he had placed under his head and set it up as a pillar and poured oil on top of it. He called that place Bethel.' Genesis 28:10–19

Bethel, probably the modern Tell Beitin 12 miles/19km north of Jerusalem, was later to play a major role in Israel's history: the resting-place of the ark of the covenant, a sanctuary visited by Samuel and later adopted by Jeroboam as a sanctuary for the northern kingdom to rival Jerusalem.

Jacob had been forced to leave home by the hot anger of his brother Esau, whom he had cheated. On his journey he found himself in an area of steep, stony, forbidding hills and valleys. 'Bethel' means 'House of God'. At first sight it can hardly have seemed that to a lonely, miserable young man leaving home. But in his dream the stony hill became a staircase filled with the messengers of God. In the morning the rock which was his pillow was set up as an altar to God. For at Bethel God renewed the promise made to Jacob's grandfather.

This event is one of the several key points in the Genesis story when God revealed himself as close and accessible to his people, not remote and uncaring. Jesus used the dream of the stairway to convey how his own coming opened up the way to the Father: 'You shall see . . . angels ascending and descending upon the Son of man'.

The Midianites, among whom Moses spent the middle years of his life, were a desert people who inhabited a region from east of the River Jordan south to the Gulf of Aqabah. Just where in this area Moses lived is not known, but certainly his wanderings with the flock on this occasion took him deep into the Sinai peninsula. 'Horeb, the mountain of God' is another name for Mount Sinai, so that Moses' call took place in the same place where he was later to receive the law.

2
FREEDOM AND A NEW LIFE

The call of Moses

'Now Moses was tending the flock of Jethro his father-in-law, the priest of Midian, and he led the flock to the far side of the desert and came to Horeb, the mountain of God. There the angel of the Lord appeared to him in flames of fire from within a bush. Moses saw that though the bush was on fire it did not burn up. So Moses thought, "I will go over and see this strange sight – why the bush does not burn up." When the Lord saw that he had gone over to look, God called to him from within the bush, "Moses, Moses!" And Moses said, "Here I am."' Exodus 3:1-4

The 'children of Israel', Jacob's descendants, sought relief from famine in Egypt. But there they found not only bread, but slavery. Who would champion their cause, and lead them to freedom from the tyranny of the Pharaoh?

Moses was far from the court of Pharaoh, the place of his upbringing. Taking the law into his own hands, he had struck a blow for his people's freedom – but the only result was his own retreat to the wilderness. But the years spent in the household of Jethro the Midianite were not wasted. This was where he gained the toughness and resources that court life could never have given him. Here he gained the knowledge of the Sinai peninsula, the Negev Desert and Transjordan which were to guide him through Israel's wilderness years.

It was here, many years later, that God revealed himself to Moses: the God of his fathers, who revealed his name to him as 'Yahweh' (Jehovah), meaning 'I AM WHO I AM'. God is the self-existent one from whom we all gain our true identity. He had felt the pain of Israel's slavery. Now he had a plan to deliver them. The first step of this plan was to call Moses and equip him to be the instrument of his people's deliverance.

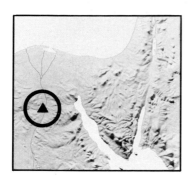

Locusts, insects not unlike the more familiar grasshopper, swarm at a particular stage in their life-cycle, when conditions are favourable. A large swarm can devour everything in its path over a vast area. The deserts of Arabia are one of their chief swarming grounds, so this prolonged east wind would have brought them into Egypt over the Red Sea.

A plague of locusts

'So Moses stretched out his staff over Egypt, and the Lord made an east wind blow across the land all that day and all that night. By morning the wind had brought the locusts; they invaded all Egypt and settled down in every area of the country in great numbers. Never before had there been such a great plague of locusts, nor will there ever be again. They covered all the ground until it was black. They devoured all that was left after the hail – everything growing in the fields and the fruit on the trees. Nothing green remained on tree or plant in all the land of Egypt.'
Exodus 10:13–15

Pharaoh would not let the people of Israel go. One plague followed another. Pharaoh realized only too well that he was fighting God himself. But he only hardened his heart still further. And the great natural catastrophes went on, one inexorably leading on to the next: an abnormally high Nile, bringing down red earth and deadly bacteria, would kill the fish. Frogs left the polluted river to plague the land, and from their rotting carcases came plagues of mosquitoes, flies and the cattle pest on the cattle in the fields. So it went on: the locusts were blown in on the wind to devastate the land afresh. Pharaoh – a god to his people because of his apparent control over the regular seasons of the Nile – was no match for the Lord of heaven and earth.

Finally, when the firstborn sons of Egypt died and the Israelites were spared on Passover night, Pharaoh let his subject people go. His last desperate change of mind led to defeat in the waters of the Red Sea, or Sea of Reeds. The exodus was the victory to which the Old Testament faith constantly looked back – though its immediate aftermath was forty tough years in the wilderness.

The Sinai peninsula is mountainous, rocky desert. Temperatures soar under the hot sun. But the whole forty years were not spent in waterless wastes such as this. There were long stays at oases, particularly Kadesh-barnea in the Negev desert.

The wilderness

'The people were thirsty for water there, and they grumbled against Moses. They said, "Why did you bring us up out of Egypt to make us and our children and livestock die of thirst?" Then Moses cried out to the Lord . . .' Exodus 17:3, 4

The glorious deliverance from Egypt was soon forgotten as the people faced the harsh realities of life in the wilderness of Sinai, short of water and food. But God showed that he would sustain those he saved: he guided Moses to the water-bearing rock at Horeb. He sent quails, flocks of migrating birds easy to catch for food. He sent manna, a small, white, honey-tasting substance. These provisions sustained them not only for the initial crossing of the wilderness, but on through the whole forty years to which their disobedience condemned them.

Tempted for forty days in another wilderness, Jesus took on his lips the key phrases of the experience of Israel: including the fact that man does not live by bread alone, but by 'every word that comes from the mouth of God'.

Sinai

'On the morning of the third day there was thunder and lightning, with a thick cloud over the mountain, and a very loud trumpet blast. Everyone in the camp trembled. Then Moses led the people out of the camp to meet with God, and they stood at the foot of the mountain.' Exodus 19:16, 17

In the third month after leaving Egypt, the Israelites came to the plain below Mount Sinai. It was to be a place of great significance for the rest of Old Testament history. Here God entered into a solemn agreement, or covenant, with his people. Their side of the agreement was to keep his commandments. These centred on the Ten Commandments, but also contained detailed instructions on how to live. They gave a pattern of morality of universal significance. The God of holiness was also a God of love, infinitely concerned for the welfare of his people.

Sanctuary in the wilderness

'The Lord said to Moses, ". . . have them make a sanctuary for me, and I will dwell among them. Make this tabernacle and all its furnishings exactly like the pattern I will show you. Have them make a chest of acacia wood – two and a half cubits long, a cubit and a half wide, and a cubit and a half high. Overlay it with pure gold, both inside and out . . . Make a table of acacia wood . . . Make a lampstand of pure gold . . ."' Exodus 25

The tabernacle, or tent, which was to be God's sanctuary in the wilderness, was modelled on other portable sanctuaries known to us from Egyptian illustrations. Clear instructions were given about how it was to be carried (on the shoulders of the Levites) and where it was to be erected (in the centre of the camp, with the tents of the various tribes ranged round it).

Many of the details symbolized the relationship of God to his people, and in this way the tabernacle was to be the model for the temple built hundreds of years later. But the instructions were also practical. The hardy acacia tree gave the wood. The gold would have been beaten from the plunder taken out of Egypt; silver, jewellery, linen and other materials also brought from Egypt; the main goat-hair covering made from the skins of their flocks.

The acacia tree, specified as the material for the wooden parts of the sanctuary, was one of the very few available in the desert – as it still is today in the Negev desert and the Sinai peninsula.

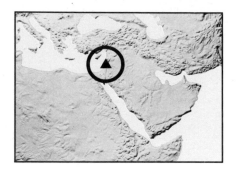

A pagan altar

'The Lord said to Moses, "Speak to the Israelites and say to them: 'I am the Lord your God. You must not do as they do in Egypt, where you used to live, and you must not do as they do in the land of Canaan, where I am bringing you' . . . *Say to the Israelites: 'Any Israelite or any alien living in Israel who gives any of his children to Molech must be put to death. The people of the community are to stone him. I will set my face against that man and I will cut him off from his people; for by giving his children to Molech, he has defiled my sanctuary and profaned my holy name . . .'"'* Leviticus 18:1–3; 20:2, 3

The law was given not only to guide Israel in their wilderness life, but also for their future settled existence in the promised land. And it was necessary for more than a good ordering of social life – it guarded their very survival. The idolatrous religion which was to surround them in Canaan was appallingly corrupt. It featured cruelties such as child sacrifice, sexual excesses such as ritual prostitution. Not surprisingly, the evil of their worship carried over into everyday life.

God's concern to keep his people from moral pollution was no mere sentiment. It was a life-and-death struggle. If Israel turned to the practices of their neighbours, it would be the end of God's whole plan for salvation for them and for the world. Total corruption and depravity can be worse even than physical death. The destruction of the Canaanites was not a matter of racial purity but of judgement on utter corruption. Right from the very beginning of their national life, the Israelites were to learn that right worship and pure living were rivetted together. They were to have nothing to do with the horrors by which the land had been profaned so long.

The picture is of an altar to the god Moloch, or Molech, at Byblos, Lebanon. The stone enclosure was for child sacrifice. Nearby stand receptacles for blood and for the rest of the disgusting pagan ritual.

A law of love

'The Lord said to Moses, "Speak to the entire assembly of Israel and say to them: 'Be holy, because I, the Lord your God, am holy . . . Do not steal. Do not lie. Do not deceive one another. Do not swear falsely by my name and so profane the name of your God. I am the Lord. Do not defraud your neighbour or rob him. Do not hold back the wages of a hired man overnight. Do not curse the deaf or put a stumbling-block in front of the blind, but fear your God. I am the Lord. Do not pervert justice; do not show partiality to the poor or favouritism to the great, but judge your neighbour fairly. Do not go about spreading slander among your people. Do not do anything that endangers your neighbour's life. I am the Lord.'"' Leviticus 19:1, 11–16

The commandments God gives to the people are rooted in his own holy character: the refrain in this passage is not 'This is how life works best', but 'I am the Lord'.

The law was moral, ceremonial and social. Detailed laws of food and hygiene reflect the climate and other local conditions in their concern for the people's health. Laws were designed to promote social justice, to safeguard the weak against exploitation by the rich, to protect those who could not protect themselves. Laws for the use of the land were designed for its conservation and highest productivity. The local applications may not be relevant in other countries and at other times, but the basic concern must be the same: loving the Lord our God must result in loving our neighbour as ourselves. The instructions given in a passage like this all point to principles which can be worked out in every society and in every age.

A law for every home

In literal obedience to the command, Jewish households have traditionally put this passage and the similar one in Deuteronomy 11:13-21 in a box attached to the door-post. Called a 'Mezuzah', it has been in use for many centuries as a physical reminder that the law must be central in the Jewish household.

'Hear, O Israel: The Lord our God, the Lord is one. Love the Lord your God with all your heart and with all your soul and with all your strength. These commandments which I give you today are to be upon your hearts . . . Write them on the door-frames of your houses and on your gates.'
Deuteronomy 6:4-6, 9

Throughout the Bible, godly living is seen as a family thing. Right from the institution of the Passover, when the children of the household had set questions to ask about the meaning of the service, the children were included in an active way in the faith and obedience of the family. The whole life of the home was to be centred on God and his ways.

The King's Highway

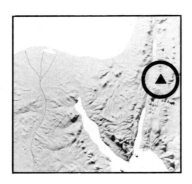

The King's Highway was already an old route by Moses' time. It was a north-south track, running to the east of the Jordan, the Dead Sea and the rift valley, whose southern end was at the Gulf of Aqabah.

'Moses sent messengers from Kadesh to the king of Edom . . . "Please let us pass through your country. We will not go through any field or vineyard, or drink water from any well. We will travel along the king's highway and not turn to the right or to the left until we have passed through your territory."' Numbers 20:14, 17

The picture shows the view the messengers would have had, looking across to the mountains of Edom. Moses' plan was to strike across to the main highway which ran through Edomite territory; but Edom would not have it. The Edomites, traditionally descended from Esau, were particularly hostile to Israel, but none of the nations of the region was friendly to the new arrivals. Israel's coming was sure to disturb the whole balance of the area, in ways they could not foresee. The only way in was to be by conquest. The frustration and constant delay and further wandering in the desert must have seemed interminable.

Jericho

'On the seventh day, they got up at daybreak and marched round the city seven times in the same manner . . . The seventh time round, when the priests sounded the trumpet blast, Joshua commanded the people, "Shout! For the Lord has given you the city!"' Joshua 6:15, 16

The forty years of wandering in the desert were over. The entry into the promised land was from the east, across Jordan. But the Israelites' problems were by no means over. They could not simply move in and occupy the land. Already they had defeated the tribes of Transjordan, and now Jericho was the first of several cities to be taken. The stories in the books of Joshua and Judges show a gradual conquest and settlement of the land.

Joshua was Moses' appointed successor, whose task was to lead Israel in the conquest of Canaan. From his commissioning as leader, it is clear that his role was not to be exactly the same as his predecessor's. Moses had found God's guidance for his leadership of the people directly, at the 'tent of meeting'. Joshua had to learn God's will through an intermediary, Eleazar, Aaron's successor as high priest. We learn much less of Joshua's character and inner struggles than we do of Moses, but certainly he was an able leader, and capable of inspiring the people to keep faithful to the task of conquest. The speeches at the beginning and end of the book named after him are moving and perceptive.

Jericho owed its position to its water-supply – the well that featured later in the story of Elisha. The mound of ancient Jericho, topped by the white hut, has remains going back to long before Joshua's time: it had already been destroyed and rebuilt several times, and as it was allowed to remain in ruins for centuries after Israel's attack it was unlikely to provide direct evidence of this actual incident. However, much that has been found there gives a commentary on many centuries of Old Testament history.

Gezer

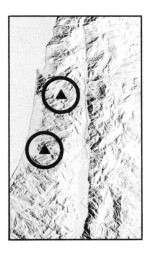

Among extensive ruins at Gezer from Joshua's time is a complex water tunnel. Other ruins remain from the time of Solomon, who rebuilt the city. Among the objects discovered was the Gezer Calendar, a simple aid for remembering the agricultural seasons (now in the Istanbul Archaeological Museum).

'Meanwhile Horam king of Gezer had come up to help Lachish, but Joshua defeated him and his army – until no survivors were left. Then Joshua and all Israel with him moved on from Lachish to Eglon; they took up positions against it and attacked it. They captured it that same day and put it to the sword and totally destroyed everyone in it, just as they had done to Lachish.'
Joshua 10:33–35

After attacking the cities near Jericho, Joshua cut across to the key fortified cities in the foothills of the mountains guarding the main highway on the plain: Lachish (see page 92) and Gezer. King Horam's sally to aid Lachish was exceptional. Generally Joshua's campaign was made much simpler by being confronted by a series of independent cities, each under its own king, who failed completely to co-operate in resisting the invader.

Megiddo

'These are the kings of the land that Joshua and the Israelites conquered on the west side of the Jordan . . . the king of Jericho . . . the king of Megiddo . . . thirty-one kings in all.'
Joshua 12:7, 9, 21, 24

At the major archaeological site of Megiddo (see too page 88), in one of the lowest layers uncovered, is this Canaanite altar or 'high place'. Called high places because they were originally on hill-tops, these pagan sanctuaries were a central feature of Canaanite religion. They were frequently condemned by the prophets, but their use or destruction by the Israelites seems to have been an accurate indication of how loyal or disloyal the people were to God at different periods of their history.

The 1,850ft/564m Mount Tabor in Galilee, with its commanding views and distinctive rounded shape, was the scene of this confrontation with the Canaanite general Sisera.

Mount Tabor

'Then Deborah said to Barak, "Go! This is the day the Lord has given Sisera into your hands. Has not the Lord gone ahead of you?" So Barak went down Mount Tabor, followed by ten thousand men. At Barak's advance, the Lord routed Sisera and all his chariots and army by the sword . . .' Judges 4:14, 15

In the period of the Judges a pattern recurs: the people turn away from God; they suffer judgement in the form of invasion or enemy occupation; they cry to God for help; he raises up a deliverer to free them. Gideon and Samson were such deliverers, but the first mentioned is Deborah. The secret of their effectiveness lay in their ability to pull the scattered tribes together into national unity. The same ebb and flow of judgement and repentance can be seen right through the time of the kings.

Deborah's magnificent song of triumph tells what happened. It seems that a sudden cloudburst turned the Kishon brook into a raging torrent, which swept many of Sisera's chariots away. The rest, clogged in the mud, would have been an easy prey.

Gideon

'Early in the morning, Gideon and all his men camped at the spring of Harod. The camp of Midian was north of them in the valley near the hill of Moreh.' Judges 7:1

So the drama of Gideon's attack on the hosts of the Midianites unfolds. Down in the valley below the slopes of Gilboa the pools from the waters of the spring Harod reflect the sky. There Gideon reduced his army to a small, crack fighting-force. The hill of Moreh opposite marks the place in the valley where the army of Midian was encamped – and where Gideon led his surprise attack.

Shechem

'Then all the citizens of Shechem and Beth Millo gathered beside the great tree at the pillar in Shechem to crown Abimelech king. When Jotham was told about this, he climbed up on the top of Mount Gerizim and shouted to them, "Listen to me, citizens of Shechem, so that God may listen to you. One day the trees went out to anoint a king for themselves . . ."' Judges 9:6–8

Shechem lay in the valley between the two mountains mentioned in Deuteronomy – Mount Ebal, to the north, on which Moses set a curse, and Mount Gerizim, to the south, the mount of blessing. Excavations have revealed buildings going back to Canaanite times, including this wall and gateway.

At Shechem Abraham camped by 'the oak of Moreh'. Here Jacob buried the 'strange gods', and Joseph sought his brothers. It was the central place where Joshua gathered the elders, just before his death. But in the time of the Judges, Shechem was still a centre of Canaanite worship. A temple to Baal was destroyed in this story, after Jotham had used his parable to attempt to turn the people from Abimelech. Later in Israel's history the northern tribes rejected Rehoboam as their king at Shechem, after Solomon's death. Jeroboam I made the town his capital for a time. After the exile it became the chief city of the Samaritans, whose sacrifices were made on nearby Mount Gerizim.

Bethlehem

'So Naomi returned from Moab accompanied by Ruth the Moabitess, her daughter-in-law, arriving in Bethlehem as the barley harvest was beginning. . . . One day Naomi her mother-in-law said to her, "My daughter, should I not try to find a home for you, where you will be well provided for? Is not Boaz, with whose servant girls you have been, a kinsman of ours? Tonight he will be winnowing barley on the threshing-floor. Wash and perfume yourself, and put on your best clothes. Then go down to the threshing-floor . . ."'
Ruth 1:22; 3:1–3

Naomi, with her husband and family, had been forced to flee from Bethlehem into the territory of Moab to escape famine. There her husband died, as did her son who had married 'Ruth the Moabitess'. The story that follows is on a totally different scale from the epic accounts in the surrounding Old Testament books. It combines lyrical simplicity and restraint with real nobility of character. Ruth shows total loyalty to her widowed mother-in-law: 'Where you go I will go, and where you stay I will stay. Your people will be my people, and your God my God'. Her kinsman honours his responsibilities towards Ruth. And only at the end of the story do we discover that these were the ancestors of King David himself, and hence the forebears of Jesus who was born in Bethlehem, city of David. The story is set in the period of the Judges, and in its simple beauty shows that life was not all war and upheaval, but also had room for the normality and honesty of ordinary rural communities.

Bethlehem, 'house of bread', straddles a ridge high in the hills of Judea. It was a quite unimportant town in the Old Testament story, although Rachel's tomb was nearby. Its fame springs entirely from its connection with Jesse and his son David, whom God 'chose to be king'.

3
A NATION UNDER GOD

Shiloh

'The boy Samuel ministered before the Lord under Eli. In those days the word of the Lord was rare; there were not many visions. One night Eli, whose eyes were becoming so weak that he could barely see, was lying down in his usual place. The lamp of God had not yet gone out, and Samuel was lying down in the temple of the Lord, where the ark of God was. Then the Lord called Samuel. Samuel answered, "Here I am." . . . The Lord was with Samuel as he grew up, and he let none of his words fall to the ground. And all Israel from Dan to Beersheba recognized that Samuel was attested as a prophet of the Lord. The Lord continued to appear at Shiloh, and there he revealed himself to Samuel through his word.' 1 Samuel 3:1–4, 19–21

As the occupation of Canaan began to get established, it was at Shiloh that the tabernacle was set up. But by Eli's time it had become some kind of temple. Here Hannah, childless and 'deeply troubled . . . poured out her soul to the Lord', vowing to dedicate her child to the Lord if he should answer her prayer. So it was that the boy Samuel grew up in the temple, and, while there, was called to be a prophet of God at a time when 'the word of the Lord was rare'.

Prophecy was a continuing feature of Old Testament religion. The first biblical character to be called a prophet was Moses, but the strand continued right through the history of the kings, taking in Elijah and Elisha, until it reached the great prophets whose words were written down, from Amos to Malachi. The emphasis was not simply on foretelling but also on 'forth-telling' – declaring the will and the judgement of God as it bore on the state of the nation from generation to generation.

Shiloh now is no more than a ruin of stones on a hill in Samaria. At the time of the Judges it was the principal sanctuary of the Israelites, but not long afterwards it was destroyed, probably by the Philistines. Jeremiah took this as an example of God's judgement on his people's wickedness.

Kiriath-Jearim

'The men of Beth Shemesh asked, "Who can stand in the presence of the Lord, this holy God? To whom will the ark go up from here?" Then they sent messengers to the people of Kiriath-Jearim, saying, "The Philistines have returned the ark of the Lord. Come down and take it up to your place." So the men of Kiriath-Jearim came and took up the ark of the Lord. They took it to Abinadab's house on the hill and consecrated Eleazar his son to guard the ark of the Lord. It was a long time, twenty years in all, that the ark remained at Kiriath-Jearim, and all the people of Israel mourned and sought after the Lord.'
1 Samuel 6:20 – 7:2

The ark was the symbol of God's presence. Captured by the Philistines, and then returned, it began its slow journey to its final resting-place in Jerusalem. A sharp reminder that God's presence is utterly holy and not to be treated casually made the men of Beth-Shemesh ask the nearby town of Kiriath-Jearim to take over the responsibility for it. From Kiriath-Jearim the ark was eventually taken to Jerusalem by David, with great rejoicing.

Commonly called 'the ark of the covenant', the ark was central to Israelite devotion. It consisted of an acacia-wood chest covered in gold, with a golden lid, sometimes called the 'mercy-seat', decorated with two cherubs. In the ark were the two stone tablets of the Ten Commandments. It was placed in the inner sanctuary of the wilderness tabernacle, then later in a tent in Jerusalem in David's time, before being solemnly transferred to Solomon's temple.

The site of Kiriath-Jearim is usually identified with the village of Abu Gosh, 9 miles/14km west of Jerusalem on the road to Jaffa. The hills above the village gave pilgrims travelling from the coast their first sight of the holy city of Jerusalem. It became customary for Jewish pilgrims to rend their clothes there to express their sorrow at the destruction of Jerusalem and its temple.

Ein Gedi

'After Saul returned from pursuing the Philistines, he was told, "David is in the Desert of En Gedi." So Saul took three thousand chosen men from all Israel and set out to look for David and his men near the Crags of the Wild Goats . . . Then David went out of the cave and called to Saul, "My lord the king!" When Saul looked behind him, David bowed down and prostrated himself with his face to the ground. He said to Saul, "Why do you listen when men say, 'David is bent on harming you'? This day you have seen with your own eyes how the Lord gave you into my hands in the cave. Some urged me to kill you, but I spared you; I said, 'I will not lift my hand against my master, because he is the Lord's anointed.'"' 1 Samuel 24:1-2, 8-10

Israel's monarchy began with Saul, but it was not an auspicious beginning. The line had to be transferred to David. Saul seemingly sensed deep down that David was the man of God's choice, and as a result, grew obsessively jealous of him. David became an outlaw, hiding in the hills and deserts to the south.

The area around Ein Gedi abounds in caves, ideal hide-outs for a hunted man. David would have had no difficulty in escaping, even from 3,000 men. He would have had no difficulty, either, in finding ready imagery for his psalms. The fresh stream in the desert surroundings, the mountains, the shadow of a mighty rock, the water cascading down cataracts and waterfalls, the gazelles and wild goats, all presented vivid pictures for his poetry.

On the west shore of the Dead Sea is a sudden burst of greenery. The fresh-water stream at Ein Gedi flows down a gorge towards the shore, making possible a patch of sub-tropical cultivation which contrasts vividly with the desert around.

The death of Saul

'Now the Philistines fought against Israel; the Israelites fled before them, and many fell slain on Mount Gilboa. The Philistines pressed hard after Saul and his sons, and they killed his sons Jonathan, Abinadab and Malki-Shua. The fighting grew fierce around Saul, and when the archers overtook him, they wounded him critically. Saul said to his armour-bearer, "Draw your sword and run me through, or these uncircumcised fellows will come and run me through and abuse me." But his armour-bearer was terrified and would not do it; so Saul took his own sword and fell on it . . . The next day, when the Philistines came to strip the dead, they found Saul and his three sons fallen on Mount Gilboa. They cut off his head and stripped off his armour, and they sent messengers throughout the land of the Philistines to proclaim the news in the temple of their idols and among their people. They put his armour in the temple of the Ashtoreths and fastened his body to the wall of Beth Shan.' 1 Samuel 31:1-4, 8-10

The Philistines, who inhabited the coastal area south of Mount Carmel, proved far harder to overcome than the other peoples of Canaan, and war with them was a recurring theme of Israelite life from the time of the Judges right through the years of the kings. Saul's struggles with them led ultimately to tragedy: Saul and Jonathan were slain on Mount Gilboa.

Saul's death opened the way for David to become king. The new dynasty was to be established which Samuel's anointing had foretold many years before. But David's reaction to the news was one of bitter grief. His lament in 2 Samuel 1 couples his respectful mourning for Saul with a more acutely felt personal sorrow for the loss of his friend Jonathan, from whom Saul's constant hostility had forced him to part.

Saul's body was displayed in the Philistine city of Beth Shan, an ancient city that had known long periods of Egyptian occupation. Among the important finds at Beth Shan were two temples which may have been those dedicated to Dagon and Ashtoreth in which Saul's armour was displayed. This view is from the site of Beth Shan looking towards the hills of Gilboa in the distance.

Hebron

'All the tribes of Israel came to David at Hebron and said, "We are your own flesh and blood. In the past, while Saul was king over us, you were the one who led Israel on their military campaigns. And the Lord said to you, 'You shall shepherd my people Israel, and you shall become their ruler.'" When all the elders of Israel had come to King David at Hebron, the king made a compact with them at Hebron before the Lord, and they anointed David king over Israel. David was thirty years old when he became king, and he reigned for forty years.'* 2 Samuel 5:1-4

Hebron had been the home of Abraham (see page 18). The highest town in Israel, it was now to be David's capital for seven and a half years until at last Jerusalem was taken. Later in David's reign, it was in Hebron that Absalom plotted his conspiracy against him.

Perhaps inevitably, a time of civil war followed Saul's death. But finally the tribes united to anoint David king at Hebron. There was to follow the greatest period in Israelite history. David was a most gifted leader, both in war and in government. The accounts of his life in 2 Samuel give a vivid impression of a great and very human person.

Jerusalem

'The king and his men marched to Jerusalem to attack the Jebusites . . . David then took up residence in the fortress and called it the City of David. He built up the area around it, from the supporting terraces inward. And he became more and more powerful, because the Lord God Almighty was with him.' 2 Samuel 5:6, 9-10

Looking up towards what was later to be the temple area, the view of Jerusalem from the south shows the part which was the ancient city of David. The domes above it are now those of mosques. Mount Zion may have been the whole area; today the name is given specifically to the hill on the left side of the picture (see too page 103). On the right the ground slopes away steeply to the Kidron Valley.

Tyre

Tyre, principal sea-port of Phoenicia, was important throughout the biblical period, right through to the time of Jesus, who once withdrew to 'the territory of Tyre and Sidon'. In Solomon's time, Tyre was at the height of its power, overshadowing its neighbour and rival, Sidon. Both towns had grown as a result of Phoenician sea-power. Originally an island, Tyre was linked to the land by a causeway at this time.

'When Hiram king of Tyre heard that Solomon had been anointed king to succeed his father David, he sent his envoys to Solomon, because he had always been on friendly terms with David. Solomon sent back this message to Hiram: "You know that because of the wars waged against my father David from all sides, he could not build a temple for the Name of the Lord his God until the Lord put his enemies under his feet. But now the Lord my God has given me peace on every side, and there is no adversary or disaster. I intend, therefore, to build a temple for the Name of the Lord my God, as the Lord told my father David when he said, 'Your son whom I will put on the throne in your place will build the temple for my Name.' So give orders that cedars of Lebanon be cut for me. My men will work with yours, and I will pay you for your men whatever wages you set. You know that we have no one so skilled in felling timber as the Sidonians.''' 1 Kings 5:1–6

Hiram, King of Tyre, had already supplied David with timber. Now at last David's son Solomon was to do what David had longed to do himself, build a 'house of the Lord'. The alliance with Tyre was a useful one. Solomon not only received cedar and cypress wood and gold. He was also given the services of a man to do all the bronze-casting for the new temple. In return, Hiram was given oil and wheat, also 'twenty cities in the land of Galilee' with which he was not particularly pleased.

Solomon inherited from David wide boundaries, well-developed administration and external peace. This gave him freedom to concentrate on increasing Israel's glory and prosperity, establishing a golden age. But this was done at the cost of stringent taxation and forced labour from within Israel. This sowed the seeds of the division which followed his death and was never repaired.

The enormous temple area dominates the old city of Jerusalem. The rocky top of Mount Moriah on which it was built is now incorporated in the Mosque of Omar (see picture, page 25). The wall pictured here is at the highest, south-eastern end. The recently uncovered masonry on the right may go back to the time of Jehoshaphat of Judah/Ahab of Israel. Since Solomon's time, successive generations have added, rebuilt, destroyed and built again on the site, until now the area incorporates building from Crusader, Muslim, Roman and Herodian days and further back still.

Solomon's temple

'In the four hundred and eightieth year after the Israelites had come out of Egypt, in the fourth year of Solomon's reign over Israel, in the month of Ziv, the second month, he began to build the temple of the Lord. The temple that King Solomon built for the Lord was sixty cubits long, twenty wide and thirty high. The portico at the front of the main hall of the temple extended the width of the temple, that is twenty cubits, and projected ten cubits from the front of the temple . . .'
1 Kings 6:1–3

Solomon's temple met the long yearning of the Israelites for a central focus for their devotion to the Lord. The ark of the covenant was solemnly placed in the inner sanctuary, and the unbroken round of daily sacrifices began. On the great annual festivals, the nation gathered for worship at the temple. When the northern tribes split off after Solomon's death, one of the grounds on which Judah condemned them was that their worship was invalid, because they set up alternative shrines. When at last Jerusalem fell to the Babylonians, the people exiled and the temple sacked, it seemed to them at first that true devotion to the Lord was impossible. Gradually they discovered that worship is not restricted to one place. But their longing (as is shown in Ezekiel's vision) was to return to the holy city and rebuild the temple.

Solomon's quarries

'In building the temple, only blocks dressed at the quarry were used, and no hammer, chisel or any other tool was heard at the temple site while it was being built.' 1 Kings 6:7

Why was this curious note included in the narrative? Deep below the old city of Jerusalem, a great cavern extends over 200yd/183m into the rock. The marks of the picks used to quarry out the rock can still be seen. Though so near to the temple, no sound of the underground quarrying could carry to the actual construction site above.

Solomon's wide interests

'God gave Solomon wisdom and very great insight, and a breadth of understanding as measureless as the sand on the seashore . . . He described plant life, from the cedar of Lebanon to the hyssop that grows out of walls. He also taught about animals and birds, reptiles and fish . . . King Solomon also built ships at Ezion Geber, which is now Elath in Edom, on the shore of the Red Sea . . . The weight of the gold that Solomon received yearly was six hundred and sixty-six talents, not including the revenues from merchants and traders and from all the Arabian kings . . . The whole world sought audience with Solomon to hear the wisdom God had put in his heart. Year after year, everyone who came brought a gift . . .'
1 Kings 4, 9, 10

Solomon was a man of many talents and wide interests. Jerusalem became a centre of commercial and cultural dealings over a very wide area. At Timna, near his port of Ezion-geber on the Red Sea, Solomon's copper-mines have been discovered. In a small valley, surrounded by the rocky hills of the Negev, the mines are being worked again today. On the top of the hill overlooking the site stood a watch-tower from which the king's men kept guard over those forced to labour in the copper-smelting pits, of which the remains can still be seen next to heaps of black slag. But the watch-tower speaks of the cost at which the splendour of Solomon's reign was built up. Tens of thousands of native Canaanites were impressed into abject slavery, not only for the mines but also for the building programmes in Jerusalem and many other cities. Even Israelites were recruited for forced labour, preparing the materials for the temple. Towards the end of his life, Solomon began to be more and more openly involved in worshipping the gods of other nations, preparing the way for the religious corruption of the monarchy in subsequent generations.

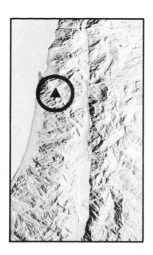

Contest on Carmel

'When Ahab saw Elijah, he said to him, "Is that you, you troubler of Israel?" . . . Ahab sent word throughout all Israel and assembled the prophets on Mount Carmel. Elijah went before the people and said, "How long will you waver between two opinions? If the Lord is God, follow him; but if Baal is God, follow him."' 1 Kings 18:17, 20, 21

Faith in the God of Israel was at a very low ebb in the reign of King Ahab. His queen Jezebel had imported hundreds of prophets of the 'Baal' from her native Phoenicia. But Elijah repeatedly challenged her and her gods. His famous challenge to Baal to bring fire on the sacrificial altar exposed the rival god at his supposed point of greatest power: control over the elements, rain and wind and fire. But God showed himself supreme. 'When all the people saw this, they fell prostrate and cried, "The Lord, he is God! The Lord, he is God!"'

A steep path leads down from the heights of Mount Carmel at its eastern end. Part-way down is a natural amphitheatre. The track goes on down to the stream at the bottom. At the top of the path there is a view of the sea in one direction, the Valley of Jezreel and Galilee in the other, Rocks litter the natural theatre. Whether or not this was the exact site of Elijah's confrontation with the prophets of Baal, the conditions are right.

Jezreel

'Naboth the Jezreelite's vineyard was in Jezreel, close to the palace of Ahab king of Samaria. Ahab said to Naboth, "Let me have your vineyard to use for a vegetable garden, since it is close to my palace . . ." But Naboth replied, "The Lord forbid that I should give you the inheritance of my fathers."' 1 Kings 21:1-3

It was Ahab's wife Jezebel who then took matters into her own hands. Naboth was quoting the law which protected the people from just such arbitrary acts of despotism and land-grabbing. But Jezebel cared nothing for the law; it took Elijah's words to reduce Ahab to repentance – and God's judgement to put an end to Jezebel's evil influence.

Ahab's palace

'So the king died and was brought to Samaria, and they buried him there. They washed the chariot at a pool in Samaria (where the prostitutes bathed) and the dogs licked up his blood, as the word of the Lord had declared. As for the other events of Ahab's reign, including all he did, the palace he built and inlaid with ivory, and the cities he fortified, are they not written in the book of the annals of the kings of Israel?'
1 Kings 22:37–39

King Omri bought a hill, and built on it the magnificent hill-top city of Samaria, which he made the capital of the kingdom of Israel. It was the northern kingdom's capital built on a site of great strategic importance. Ahab erected a temple there to the Tyrian Baal, and then built a luxurious palace. More than 200 pieces of ivory were discovered in a storeroom, during the excavation of the site.

None of the kings of Israel stayed loyal to God, and the interplay of alliances, as well as inherited enmity, often brought them into conflict with Judah. Through the generations, different prophets rose up to challenge the luxury, injustice and idolatry of Samaritan society, from Elijah and Elisha to the first two 'writing prophets', Amos and Hosea. About a hundred years after Ahab's death, Amos tells of people who 'feel secure on Mount Samaria . . . who lie on beds inlaid with ivory', and goes on to depict their downfall.

The picture shows the remains of Ahab's palace, high up on the hill among ruins from the time of the Roman occupation, centuries later. A pool, 10yd/9m long, probably the one in which Ahab's blood-stained chariot was washed down, has also been uncovered.

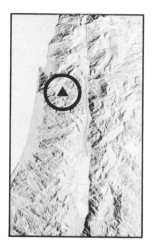

The chariot cities

'Now Ben-Hadad king of Aram mustered his entire army. Accompanied by thirty-two kings with their horses and chariots, he went up and besieged Samaria and attacked it. He sent messengers into the city to Ahab king of Israel, saying, "This is what Ben-Hadad says: 'Your silver and gold are mine, and the best of your wives and children are mine.'"' 1 Kings 20:1–3

The threat of Ben-Hadad, for all his bravado, was fought off, both in the hills and later on the plain. Chariots featured, too, in Ahab's battle with Shalmaneser III at Qarqar: according to Shalmaneser, Ahab had a force of 2,000 chariots. The picture shows the remains of the stables for his horses at Megiddo. Solomon had established Megiddo, Hazor and Gezer as chariot cities, built to an identical plan: 'he had fourteen hundred chariots and twelve thousand horses, which he kept in the chariot cities and also with him in Jerusalem' (1 Kings 10:26). Built to guard the pass through the Carmel range on the main north-south coastal highway, Megiddo reflects layer after layer of Bible history (see too page 51). Here King Josiah was killed attempting to halt Egyptian forces on their way to aid crumbling Assyria. By New Testament times, Megiddo had seen so many battles that the writer of Revelation could use its name 'Armaggedon' (or 'Har Magedon', the Hill of Megiddo) as a symbol of war.

Water-troughs and hitching-posts from Megiddo, at the Rockefeller Museum, Jerusalem.

The siege of Samaria

*'The king of Assyria invaded the entire land,
marched against Samaria and laid siege to it for
three years. In the ninth year of Hoshea, the king
of Assyria captured Samaria and deported the
Israelites to Assyria . . . All this took place
because the Israelites had sinned against the Lord
their God, who had brought them out of Egypt
from under the power of Pharaoh king of Egypt.
They worshipped other gods, and followed the
practices of the nations the Lord had driven out
before them, as well as the practices which the
kings of Israel had introduced. The Israelites
secretly did things against the Lord their God that
were not right . . .'* 2 Kings 17:5-9

The threat from Assyria, for so long just over
the horizon, became an ugly reality. The
crumbling walls on the heights of Samaria look
down over a scene which, in 722 BC, saw the
culmination of three years of siege. The city
fell. The people were deported. The area was
repopulated by Assyria with other conquered
peoples. These intermarried with the few
Israelites who were left, forming the Samaritan
people so despised and hated in the time of
Jesus, and surviving today as a few hundred
people with their own traditions and worship.

The prophets had warned the people of the
coming invasion, warned them to turn from
their sin and from the judgement to come. The
northern kingdom was never to be re-
established. The line of God's promise was now
limited to the southern kingdom of Judah. One
of the great themes of the prophets was thus
historically vindicated: that God's judgement is
not an idle threat. A nation cannot continue to
flout the law of God and expect to remain
strong and secure. Real security lies, not in
military strength and alliances, but in
conforming the life of the people to the
declared will of God.

Lachish

'In the fourteenth year of King Hezekiah's reign, Sennacherib king of Assyria attacked all the fortified cities of Judah and captured them. So Hezekiah king of Judah sent this message to the king of Assyria at Lachish: "I have done wrong. Withdraw from me, and I will pay whatever you demand of me." The king of Assyria exacted from Hezekiah king of Judah three hundred talents of silver and thirty talents of gold. So Hezekiah gave him all the silver that was found in the temple of the Lord and in the treasuries of the royal palace.'
2 Kings 18:13–16

Eight years after the fall of Samaria and the exile of the northern kingdom of Israel, the Assyrians attacked Judah to the south. Lachish, a fortified city in the foothills of Judah in the approaches to Jerusalem, had first to be immobilized before the capital itself. In the years of the conquest, Joshua had taken Lachish in an attack lasting two days: signs of burning from that time can still be seen. The fortifications were strengthened under Rehoboam. But now they faced a formidable and quite ruthless war-machine. Assyria was not like the petty kingdoms Judah had resisted before. The siege by the Assyrian general Sennacherib was vividly portrayed in reliefs on the walls of his palace at Nineveh (now in the British Museum). Hezekiah paid heavy tribute but it made no difference. With Lachish wiped out and the lines of support from Egypt thus cut off, Sennacherib marched on Jerusalem.

The 'tell', or mound, covering the remains of ancient Lachish can be seen in the background of the picture opposite. The picture above shows the remains on top of the mound. The heavy destruction caused by Sennacherib's armies is shown in the remains discovered by archaeologists – and a mass grave holding 1,500 bodies.

The defence of Jerusalem

'Then Isaiah said to Hezekiah, "Hear the word of the Lord: The time will surely come when everything in your palace, and all that your fathers have stored up until this day, will be carried off to Babylon. Nothing will be left, says the Lord . . ." As for the other events of Hezekiah's reign, all his achievements and how he made the pool and the tunnel by which he brought water into the city, are they not written in the book of the annals of the kings of Judah? Hezekiah rested with his fathers. And Manasseh his son succeeded him as king.'
2 Kings 20:16–17, 20–21

As king of Judah, Hezekiah had initiated thorough and widespread reforms. He reopened the temple and established its services, attacked pagan practices, undertook extensive rebuilding and the fortification of Jerusalem against the threat of invasion. With Josiah, fifty years before, he is one of the handful of kings of Judah to emerge with credit from the accounts in the Old Testament histories. One of his measures was to ensure that the people of Jerusalem had access to a water supply in time of siege. This proved highly important when Sennacherib invaded the city, and despite all the blustering threats of the invading army, Jerusalem held out until the Assyrians were overtaken by calamity and dispersed. It was a reprieve. The city was to have more than a century of continued life before the next imperial power, Nebuchadnezzar of Babylon, attacked and destroyed the city in 587 BC.

Hezekiah had a tunnel dug from the Gihon spring, pictured here, 1,750ft/533m through solid rock to the Pool of Siloam inside the walls. The tunnel was discovered in 1880, including an inscription (now in the Istanbul Archaeological Museum) graphically recording the day when the excavating teams from each side of the rock barrier met in the middle.

Most of the present walls of Jerusalem date from medieval times. Some of the massive masonry survives from Herod's temple, started in 19 BC and finished only a few years before its destruction by the Romans in AD 70. The picture below shows the 'Golden Gate' in the position of the one east-facing gate of Herod's temple.

Return to Jerusalem

'I went to Jerusalem, and after staying there three days I set out during the night with a few men. I had not told anyone what my God had put in my heart to do for Jerusalem . . . Then I said to them, "You see the trouble we are in: Jerusalem lies in ruins, and its gates have been burned with fire. Come, let us rebuild the wall of Jerusalem, and we will no longer be in disgrace." I also told them about the gracious hand of my God upon me and what the king had said to me. They replied, "Let us start rebuilding."'
Nehemiah 2:11–12, 17–18

All the leading inhabitants were taken off to Babylon following Jerusalem's fall. They left behind a ruined city and a demoralized remnant population. Their seventy years of exile were in some ways a refining process, and their sense of religious and national identity stayed intact. When the Babylonians were overthrown by the Medes and Persians, an empire took control whose policy was to allow local autonomy. The Jews were permitted to return. Isaiah's prophecy that 'the ransomed of the Lord will return' began to come true. But the re-establishment of a derelict city and society takes leadership, and many years were still to pass before Jerusalem's morale began to revive.

Nehemiah in exile was cupbearer to the king of Persia. In this influential position he was able to take action following reports he had heard of the state of Jerusalem. A man of prayer, he was also a man of great organizational ability. Despite opposition, under his leadership the people rebuilt the walls of Jerusalem in under two months. Nehemiah was appointed governor in 445 BC, went back to Persia for a time, and returned later to reform abuses that had arisen in his absence. With Ezra, he re-established worship and obedience to the law of God.

4
POETS AND PROPHETS

Job

'In the land of Uz there lived a man whose name was Job. This man was blameless and upright; he feared God and shunned evil. He had seven sons and three daughters, and he owned seven thousand sheep, three thousand camels, five hundred yoke of oxen and five hundred donkeys, and had a large number of servants. He was the greatest man among all the people of the East. His sons used to take turns holding feasts in their homes, and they would invite their three sisters to eat and drink with them. When a period of feasting had run its course, Job would send and have them purified. Early in the morning he would sacrifice a burnt offering for each of them, thinking, "Perhaps my children have sinned and cursed God in their hearts." This was Job's regular custom.'
Job 1:1–5

The book of Job is a haunting poetic drama. We do not know who wrote it, or when and where it was written. It is tempting to think it was the product of fireside storytelling, told and retold since the patriarchal times in which it was set. It may, however, have arisen out of the much more sophisticated environment that also produced Proverbs and Ecclesiastes, as an intellectual protest against the religious dogmatism and blinkered theology which reduced God to a set of rules. The drama unfolds to show that all the traditional answers to the age-old problem of suffering were wide of the mark. It seemed obvious to Job's comforters that when he lost his wealth and his ten children and was stricken with illness, it was God judging him for his sins. But that was not so. Job's eventual encounter with God in his majesty takes him right to the heart of the mystery of existence.

The Lord is my Shepherd

'The Lord is my shepherd,
I shall lack nothing.
He makes me lie down in green pastures,
he leads me beside quiet waters,
he restores my soul.
He guides me in paths of righteousness
for his name's sake.
Even though I walk through the valley
of the shadow of death,
I will fear no evil,
for you are with me;
your rod and your staff,
they comfort me . . .'
Psalm 23

The Psalms were both Israel's hymn-book and her anthology of poetry. They include hymns for religious occasions, such as the 'songs of ascents', sung by the worshippers in procession behind the ark as they climbed the hill to the temple at a festival. Others were for the coronations of Israel's kings. Others again had titles suggesting they were for thanksgiving or lament or teaching. Often they look back to the great events of Israel's past for evidence of God's greatness. One of the reasons people through the centuries have identified so closely with the Psalms is that many are very personal, the expression of trust, or despair, or joy, or wonder; they contain great depth and honesty of emotion.

A picture of sheep grazing in lush meadows beside still waters is not an easy one to find in the lands of the Middle East. It was an ideal, a beautiful picture of peace and security. For the one whose shepherd is God himself it can be realized even in conditions which are less than ideal – even among enemies and facing the threat of danger and death.

Gazelles on the mountains

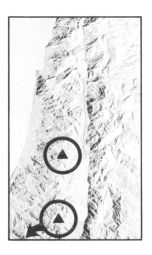

These gazelles are in the gorge of Avdat, in the Negev desert in the south of Israel. Hart, or deer, are no longer to be found in Israel – the last disappeared early this century.

'As the deer pants for streams of water,
so my soul pants for you, O God.
My soul thirsts for God, for the living God.
When can I go and meet with God?
My tears have been my food day and night,
while men say to me all day long,
"Where is your God?"'
Psalm 42:1–3

The Psalms are rich in imagery from the countryside and desert: not only deer but sheep, lions, birds, coneys; not only animals but cedar trees, rocks, streams, hills and fields in harvest. This psalm uses a universal religious image – the desert, where it is only too easy to appreciate the aching longing for water expressed by the psalmist. He has been forced to leave the temple, and he longs for its worship. It is a time of real darkness, but also of hope: 'Why are you downcast, O my soul? Why so disturbed within me? Put your hope in God, for I will yet praise him, my Saviour and my God.'

Mount Zion

'Great is the Lord, and most worthy of praise,
in the city of our God, his holy mountain . . .
Walk about Zion, go round her,
count her towers,
consider well her ramparts,
view her citadels,
that you may tell of them to the next generation.
For this God is our God for ever and ever.'
Psalm 48:1, 12–14

Mount Zion was one of the hills of Jerusalem. Traditionally the name has been referred to the one pictured here; but David's City itself was further to the east, and it is clear that Zion included the religious centre of Israel, the temple. So it is often used as a general name for Jerusalem.

Massada, the fortress

*'He who dwells in the shelter of the Most High
will rest in the shadow of the Almighty.
I will say of the Lord, "He is my refuge and my
fortress,
my God, in whom I trust.". . .
His faithfulness will be your shield and rampart.
You will not fear the terror of night,
nor the arrow that flies by day,
nor the pestilence that stalks in the darkness,
nor the plague that destroys at midday.
A thousand may fall at your side,
ten thousand at your right hand,
but it will not come near you.'* Psalm 91:1-7

Just over two miles from the Dead Sea, in the rocky Wilderness of Judea, rises the great rock slab of Massada, or Metsuda, a fortress or stronghold. Here the Jews made their last heroic stand against the Romans in AD 73. After three years of siege, when the Romans were completing the massive ramp they used to storm the summit, the defenders put themselves to death rather than fall into enemy hands.

Several times in the Psalms David calls the Lord his fortress. It may have been to this place that he came when fleeing from Saul: 'David and his men went up to the stronghold.' In any case it was a powerful image of the fact that God would not only defend him but would himself be his refuge and fortress. It was one of the many ways he used to express his trust in God even when things were at their bleakest: 'God is my refuge and strength, an ever-present help in trouble.'

At Massada today can be seen storehouses, reservoirs and fortifications from the time of the Jewish Revolt; also remains of a palace built by Herod, and ruins of a Roman fort.

Wisdom in the streets

'Wisdom calls aloud in the street,
she raises her voice in the public squares;
at the head of the noisy streets she cries out,
in the gateways of the city she makes her speech:
"How long will you simple ones love your simple
ways?
How long will mockers delight in mockery
and fools hate knowledge?
If you had responded to my rebuke,
I would have poured out my heart to you
and made my thoughts known to you . . ."'
Proverbs 1:20–23

The Old Testament 'wisdom literature' includes Proverbs, Job and Ecclesiastes. Job is one great poetic drama. Ecclesiastes is a single extended reflection. But Proverbs is quite different in its literary form: a collection of short pithy thoughts. The basic concern in all three books is the same: to seek out what is true in life. In Proverbs this is expressed in 'wise sayings', conveying what is 'true in general', what accords with God's wisdom in ordinary, practical daily life. They are not so much promises from God as descriptions of what life is like under God. Idleness, falsehood, dishonesty, crooked dealing, adultery are not the way to wisdom and life. Trusting in God, living a life that is consistent with the way he has been created, this is how man has been designed to live and so the way to true success and happiness. Wisdom is so highly valued in Proverbs that it almost acquires an individual life and personality.

Overgrown vineyard

'I went past the field of the sluggard,
past the vineyard of the man who lacks judgment;
thorns had come up everywhere,
the ground was covered with weeds,
and the stone wall was in ruins.
I applied my heart to what I observed
and learned a lesson from what I saw:
A little sleep, a little slumber,
a little folding of the hands to rest –
and poverty will come on you like a bandit,
and scarcity like an armed man.'
Proverbs 24:30–34

In graphic, humorous detail the point is made. Laziness inevitably leads to ruin. Again, this is what is usually the case; it is a simple observation of life. The perils of idleness are a big theme of the sayings, and the wise man is seen as the one who makes a profit. But there are other, less pragmatic themes as well: concern for the poor, respect for the king, a high regard for marriage, a good ordering of society, honesty in commercial life.

The nations around Israel at this time also had their 'wisdom books', such as the Egyptian *Wisdom of Amenemope*, which some believe to lie behind Proverbs and others that it is derived from the same collection of Hebrew sayings. Some have concluded that the Bible's wisdom is therefore not original. But the whole point of wisdom literature was to distil what is universally true. If this has been well expressed by secular man, then its truth can be underlined. But 'wisdom' which does not relate human life to the one who created and sustains it is not truly wise; for the 'fear of the Lord is the beginning of wisdom'.

Life under the sun

' "Meaningless! Meaningless!" says the Teacher.
"Utterly meaningless! Everything is meaningless."
What does man gain from all his labour
at which he toils under the sun?
Generations come and generations go,
but the earth remains for ever.
The sun rises and the sun sets,
and hurries back to where it rises . . .
All things are wearisome,
more than one can say . . .
there is nothing new under the sun.'
Ecclesiastes 1:2–5, 8–9

Life without God is vain, empty, fruitless. The seasons come and go, nothing changes, nothing is new. In love or war, toil or leisure, life goes on, life 'under the sun' is apparently pointless, meaningless. If all this has a twentieth-century ring to it, it is not by accident. For 'the Teacher' was doing what many twentieth-century writers are also doing: expressing the cynicism and meaninglessness of man and the daily round. But Ecclesiastes also introduces a wider perspective, that of life under God. The note he sounds of quietly accepting life from God's hand is very different from most modern thinking. He scarcely begins to give answers; life is inscrutable at times and it is idle to pretend we understand it all. As the Bible makes plain, the clearer picture awaits the coming of the One who can make all things new.

Song of songs

'Dark am I, yet lovely,
O daughters of Jerusalem,
dark like the tents of Kedar,
like the tent curtains of Solomon.
Do not stare at me because I am dark,
because I am darkened by the sun.
My mother's sons were angry with me
and made me take care of the vineyards;
my own vineyard I have neglected.
Tell me, you whom I love,
where you graze your flock
and where you rest your sheep at midday.
Why should I be like a veiled woman
beside the flocks of your friends?'
Song of Songs 1:5–7

The Bible's collection of poetry and wisdom would be incomplete without the pure lyric feeling and joy in love expressed in the Song of Solomon. It is difficult to unravel the 'story' expressed in the dialogue between the bridegroom and bride. Some see it as the tale of a beautiful country girl taken to the King's court, who is torn between the royal suitor and her rustic lover. But it may be that it is simply a collection of love-songs grouped together with little connection. What is clear is that the Bible contains in this book a celebration of the purity, beauty and wonder of human love. It was Greek philosophy that introduced the idea that physical love belongs to the lower nature, and that things of the soul have no connection with things of the body. The Bible sees no such division. The God who created man to love him also created man and woman and their love for one another.

Scarlet dye

' "Come now, let us reason together,"
says the Lord.
"Though your sins are like scarlet,
they shall be as white as snow;
though they are red as crimson,
they shall be like wool." '
Isaiah 1:18

After Solomon's death, the unity and wealth of
the kingdom was disrupted by civil war and the
division of the kingdom into north and south,
Judah and Israel. By Isaiah's time, Judah under
King Uzziah was again prosperous. The danger
was not civil war or even invasion but the sins
of luxury and self-indulgence. Whatever the
danger and whatever the sin, Isaiah remained
faithful to his prophetic message, recalling men
from evil and promising God's forgiveness in
response to repentance and faith. Later in his
ministry, Isaiah saw the Assyrian armies
threatening Jerusalem. More than any other
Bible prophet, he seems to have had the ear of
the king. He encouraged Hezekiah to trust in
God and not to put store on alliances. But he
warns of the overthrow that will follow
disobedience to God.

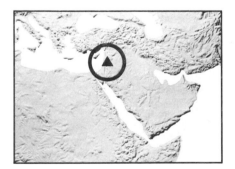

Tyre and Sidon

'Wail, O ships of Tarshish!
For Tyre is destroyed
and left without house or harbour . . .
Be ashamed, O Sidon,
and you, O fortress of the sea . . .'
Isaiah 23:1, 4

The Phoenicians of Tyre and Sidon were indeed
the merchants and seafarers of the nations.
Isaiah's prophecy about Sidon (pictured here)
came about when the Assyrians under
Sennacherib marched on the city and defeated
it. Much of Isaiah's book is concerned with the
nations around, both inveighing against their
immorality and warning of the dangers of
invasion or alliance. Because of their strategic
importance in commerce and communications,
Sidon and Tyre (pictured on page 75) continued
to be dominated by foreign powers, down to
Roman times. It was here that Jesus healed the
daughter of the Syro-Phoenician woman, and
many listened to his teaching there.

Water in the desert

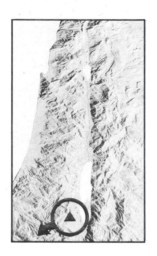

'The poor and needy search for water,
but there is none;
their tongues are parched with thirst.
But I the Lord will answer them,
I, the God of Israel, will not forsake them.
I will make rivers flow on barren heights,
and springs within the valleys.
I will turn the desert into pools of water,
and the parched ground into springs . . .
so that people may see and know,
may consider and understand,
that the hand of the Lord has done this,
that the Holy One of Israel has created it.'
Isaiah 41:17–18, 20

Isaiah brought the message that, even if the people were taken into exile, their God would never abandon them. He called them to lift up their eyes to a future in which they would return to their own land – a land restored in all its beauty, where God would dwell in harmony with his people. In a country with such a large proportion of barren desert, it was natural for the symbol of this messianic rule to become 'the desert that blossomed'. Rain is rare in the desert, but the seeds lie waiting in the soil and grow with astonishing rapidity when water does reach them, so that a parched landscape rapidly becomes green. In the same way the people will find new life and surging joy when God gives them what their hearts long for.

Gehenna

'The people of Judah have done evil in my eyes, declares the Lord. They have set up their detestable idols in the house that bears my Name and have defiled it. They have built the high places of Topheth in the Valley of Ben Hinnom to burn their sons and daughters in the fire – something I did not command nor did it enter my mind. So beware; the days are coming, declares the Lord, when people will no longer call it Topheth or the Valley of Ben Hinnom, but the Valley of Slaughter . . . I will bring an end to the sounds of joy and gladness and to the voices of bride and bridegroom in the towns of Judah and the streets of Jerusalem, for the land will become desolate.'
Jeremiah 7:30–32, 34

Jeremiah is generally associated with gloom and disaster, and this was bound to be his message, given his calling and the times in which he lived. But as a sensitive and gentle man, this was the last sort of message he wanted to bring. Occasionally the personal conflict between his vision and his inclinations comes through in his book, when he complains that the Lord's word 'is in my bones like a burning fire'.

His ministry extended over the reign of five kings of Judah, leading up to the Babylonians. Jerusalem had no lack of prophets who proclaimed '"Peace, peace," when there is no peace, says the Lord'. But Jeremiah had to be faithful to a message of God's judgement. Even when the city had become subject to Nebuchadnezzar, and a puppet king installed, he still had to warn that worse was to come. But he also had a vision of a brighter future when God would bring in 'a new covenant': his people would receive forgiveness and a restored relationship with himself.

The Valley of Hinnom, pictured here, curves round the south-western side of the city of Jerusalem. In Jeremiah's time it was associated with the evils of child-sacrifice. It was also to become the city rubbish-dump, where the refuse was continually burning. The name Hinnom, or Gehenna, became a symbol of hell itself.

The potter

'This is the word that came to Jeremiah from the Lord: "Go down to the potter's house, and there I will give you my message." So I went down to the potter's house, and I saw him working at the wheel. But the pot he was shaping from the clay was marred in his hands; so the potter formed it into another pot, shaping it as seemed best to him.

'Then the word of the Lord came to me: "O house of Israel, can I not do with you as this potter does?"' Jeremiah 18:1–6

As the lump of clay is turned on the wheel, it is formed by the potter's hand into a jar or bowl. This was a vivid picture of the way God 'moulds' his people, and one that recurs in the Bible. Equally, as here, the pot that did not shape up as intended could be scrapped and started again. 'Behold, like the clay in the potter's hand, so are you in my hand, O house of Israel.' The message can be applied to any generation, but it was specifically directed to Jeremiah's contemporaries. God had given many promises to Jerusalem and to their monarchy, that they would never fail. There was a great temptation for the people to look for false security in these promises, feeling safe from God's judgement. But the prophet knew that God intended to break the spoiled pot, and that his promises would be fulfilled in another way, at another time.

A basket of figs

*'After Jehoiachin son of Jehoiakim king of Judah
and the officials, the craftsmen and the artisans of
Judah were carried into exile from Jerusalem to
Babylon by Nebuchadnezzar king of Babylon, the
Lord showed me two baskets of figs placed in front
of the temple of the Lord. One basket had very
good figs, like those that ripen early; the other
basket had very poor figs, so bad that they could
not be eaten. Then the Lord asked me, "What do
you see, Jeremiah?" "Figs," I answered. "The
good ones are very good, but the poor ones are so
bad that they cannot be eaten."'*
Jeremiah 24:1–3

Many of the prophecies were delivered in
striking pictorial terms. This was not simply to
heighten their effect; the prophets would
actually see an image in their mind's eye and
report what they saw, together with its
interpretation. Ezekiel, in exile in Babylon, even
built models under the fascinated gaze of his
watchers.

Nebuchadnezzar had put Zedekiah on the
throne of Judah – a mere puppet-king. (The
Old Testament account of this is supported by
the Babylonian Chronicle.) The previous leaders
had been taken into exile, and the new king
surrounded himself with poor substitutes –
Jeremiah's 'good and bad figs'. The prophet
risked his neck for his outspokenness: God
would renew his covenant with his faithful,
exiled people, but Zedekiah and his princes
would be utterly destroyed. It is a forceful
example of the prophet's different scale of
vision: where his compatriots were complacent
about the present and ignored the long-term
future, Jeremiah saw only judgement near at
hand but had a clear vision of greater days far
ahead.

The pool at Gibeon

'In the seventh month Ishmael . . . came with ten men to Gedaliah son of Ahikam at Mizpah. While they were eating together there, Ishmael son of Nethaniah and the ten men who were with him got up and struck down Gedaliah son of Ahikam, the son of Shaphan, with the sword, killing the one whom the king of Babylon had appointed as governor over the land . . . When Johanan son of Kareah and all the army officers who were with him heard about all the crimes Ishmael son of Nethaniah had committed, they took all their men and went to fight Ishmael son of Nethaniah. They caught up with him near the great pool in Gibeon.'
Jeremiah 41:1–2, 11–12

Excavations at a site now called el-Jib, about 6 miles/9km north of Jerusalem revealed a large pit with stairs leading down to a tunnel. The tunnel leads to a well outside the walls of the city. In the pit were jars inscribed with the name of the city: Gibeon. The events of the 'great pool of Gibeon' were part of the tangled aftermath of the Babylonian invasion, the murder of the governor Gedaliah being followed by the counter-attack and eventual flight to Egypt – Jeremiah being unwillingly taken along with the rest. It is a squalid story and evidence of a demoralized society. The wonder is that Judah ever survived the Babylonian occupation and the decay of their social and religious standards. But the exile was to prove a time of refinement.

The Wailing Wall

'How deserted lies the city,
one so full of people!
How like a widow is she,
who once was great among the nations!
She who was queen among the provinces
has now become a slave . . .
You, O Lord, reign for ever;
your throne endures from generation to generation.
Why do you always forget us?
Why do you forsake us so long?
Restore us to yourself, O Lord, that we may
return;
renew our days as of old
unless you have utterly rejected us
and are angry with us beyond measure.'
Lamentations 1:1; 5:19–22

The beginning and end of Lamentations sum up the aspirations of a people denied their spiritual home: 'How long, O Lord . . .' The book, most of it written in the rigid, highly stylized form of an acrostic, each verse starting with a different Hebrew letter, is thought to come from the time just after the fall of Jerusalem. Its deep agony of soul has spoken to the hearts of Jews through the centuries since the later overthrow of their city by the Romans in AD 70.

The Wailing Wall, or Western Wall of the former temple in Jerusalem, has been the focus of the sorrow and hope of the dispersed people of Israel down to the present day. Since Israel's repossession of the wall it has become a shrine and symbol of national renewal.

The cedar tree

'This is what the Sovereign Lord says: "I myself will take a shoot from the very top of a cedar and plant it; I will break off a tender sprig from its topmost shoots and plant it on a high and lofty mountain. On the mountain heights of Israel I will plant it; it will produce branches and bear fruit and become a splendid cedar. Birds of every kind will nest in it; they will find shelter in the shade of its branches. All the trees of the field will know that I the Lord bring down the tall tree and make the low tree grow tall. I dry up the green tree and make the dry tree flourish. I the Lord have spoken, and I will do it."' Ezekiel 17:22–24

Ezekiel was from a priestly family. Due to embark on his priestly career when he was thirty, he was deported to Babylon at exactly that age. On the day that Jerusalem fell, his wife died. It summed up his complete personal identification with the subject of his message. With emotional intensity and vivid symbolism he expressed the concern and longing of an exile for his land and for his nation's spiritual renewal. Several of his word-pictures have become widely known: the heart of stone and the heart of flesh, the river flowing out from the sanctuary, and above all, the valley of dry bones. His oracle about the cedar of Lebanon and the eagle which took a branch from its top is typical of his soaring prophetic imagination. Today the magnificent cedars of Lebanon, once the source of timber for Solomon's temple, are reduced to a few isolated groves of trees high in the mountains.

The watchman

'Son of man, I have made you a watchman for the house of Israel; so hear the word I speak and give them warning from me. When I say to the wicked, "O wicked man, you will surely die," and you do not speak out to dissuade him from his ways, that wicked man will die for his sin, and I will hold you accountable for his blood. But if you do warn the wicked man to turn from his ways and he does not do so, he will die for his sin, but you will be saved yourself.' Ezekiel 33:7–9

With characteristic concern, Ezekiel sees his role as a matter of life and death. If as watchman he fails to warn the people of their impending fate, their blood will be on his head. Such earnestness and utter dedication was typical of the 'prophets of the Lord'; theirs was a key role, carrying heavy responsibility both to God and to his people. It is hard to imagine Judah's religious life continuing in existence without the prophets. Time and again they called the people back to an awareness of their destiny, linked inextricably with God who had called them. Particularly in the generations leading up to the fall of Jerusalem and during and immediately after the exile, it was the great prophets who kept the Jews looking on to a future hope, and who helped them to interpret what was happening to them in a way that showed God's hand was not withdrawn.

Small towers from which watchmen can keep guard over valuable crops and olive-groves are a familiar sight among the hills of Judah and Samaria.

Return, O Israel

'Return, O Israel, to the Lord your God.
Your sins have been your downfall . . .
"I will heal their waywardness
and love them freely,
for my anger has turned away from them.
I will be like the dew to Israel;
he will blossom like a lily.
Like a cedar of Lebanon
he will send down his roots;
his young shoots will grow.
His splendour will be like an olive tree,
his fragrance like a cedar of Lebanon.
Men will dwell again in his shade.
He will flourish like the grain.
He will blossom like a vine,
and his fame will be like the wine from
Lebanon. "'
Hosea 14:1, 4–7

Hosea was another prophet deeply identified with his message. As a northerner, he loved the land and its gentle landscapes, like this peaceful scene in Galilee. He also loved his wife, and it was her unfaithfulness which showed him how agonizing it was to God that his people should be unfaithful and rebellious. All that God had given them, in the fruitfulness of their land, he saw them wrongly attributing to the bounty of the local Canaanite fertility gods – the Baals. It was as though they were taking the idols as lovers, as the prophet's wife was doing to his own personal humiliation. Hosea spelt out the indulgence and social injustice of his society. But his deepest concern was to show God's love for his people, his longing to forgive them, his longing to restore them to the peace and content expressed in the picture of lily and cedar, olive and vine.

The ploughman

' "The days are coming," declares the Lord,
"when the reaper shall be overtaken by the
ploughman
and the planter by the one treading grapes.
New wine will drip from the mountains
and flow from all the hills.
I will bring back my exiled people Israel;
they will rebuild the ruined cities and live in them.
They will plant vineyards and drink their wine;
they will make gardens and eat their fruit.
I will plant Israel in their own land,
never again to be uprooted
from the land I have given them, "
says the Lord your God.'
Amos 9:13–15

Amos was a countryman, called from Tekoa in
the deep south of Judea to proclaim God's word
in the northern capital of Samaria. He was
sickened by the corruption, immorality and
inequality of the city. More than any other
prophet, Amos had a burning concern for social
righteousness; he longed for the people to 'let
justice roll on like a river, righteousness like a
never-failing stream'. He called them to
repentance, but saw his message totally ignored.
God's judgement will come, and the 'day of the
Lord', to which they looked forward as a time
when God would give them victory, was going
to be 'a day of darkness not light'. Only in these
last verses of his prophecy does he allow a hope
for the future to break through.

In rural areas of the Middle
East today a wooden plough
is still used, drawn by a
horse or by oxen.

The altar at Byblos, Lebanon, was dedicated to pagan practices going back to Canaanite times.

A pagan shrine

' "In that day," declares the Lord . . .
"I will destroy your witchcraft
and you will no longer cast spells.
I will destroy your carved images
and your sacred stones from among you;
you will no longer bow down to the work of your
hands . . ."
With what shall I come before the Lord,
and bow down before the exalted God? . . .
He has showed you, O man, what is good.
And what does the Lord require of you?
To act justly and to love mercy
and to walk humbly with your God.'
Micah 5:10, 12–13; 6:6, 8

The prophets combined demands for social justice with denunciation of the evils of pagan religion. The idolatrous cults of Israel's neighbours made no connection between worship and morality. A devotee might offer the costliest sacrifices one day and engage in the most depraved or oppressive behaviour the next. In the face of this, the consistent ground-theme of the prophets is that right worship and right living belong inseparably together. God hates the hypocrisy of religion which has no effect on life. And this is just as true of the worship of the Lord: '"The multitude of your sacrifices, what are they to me?" says the Lord . . . "Take your evil deeds out of my sight."'

Micah was a younger contemporary of Isaiah, who prophesied in the southern kingdom of Judah at about the time the northern kingdom fell to the Assyrians.

The storehouse

' "Will a man rob God? Yet you rob me. But you ask, 'How do we rob you?' In tithes and offerings. You are under a curse – the whole nation of you – because you are robbing me. Bring the whole tithe into the storehouse, that there may be food in my house. Test me in this," says the Lord Almighty, "and see if I will not throw open the floodgates of heaven and pour out so much blessing that you will not have room enough for it. I will prevent pests from devouring your crops, and the vines in your fields will not cast their fruit," says the Lord Almighty. "Then all the nations will call you blessed, for yours will be a delightful land," says the Lord Almighty.' Malachi 3:8–12

A rural economy depended to a large extent on storage of oil and grain, and the storehouse to Malachi was a test of the people's devotion to God. Then, as now, it was a question of whether the people would show where their heart was by putting their money there also. Their law stated very precisely that the 'tithe', or tenth part of all the crops and livestock they produced, was to be given to the Lord for the support of the landless Levites, dedicated to leading the people's worship. But this practice seems to have fallen into disuse, and Malachi, the last of the Old Testament prophets, calls them back to it.

Throughout Old Testament times, the choice was simple, but difficult. Will man love God with all his heart and soul and all that he is, following the ways of his law and his creation? Or will he go his own way, with all the disastrous results recorded in Old Testament history? Today the choice is as acutely necessary as ever.

The pillars of this building at Hazor, in northern Galilee, are thought to have belonged to a storehouse.

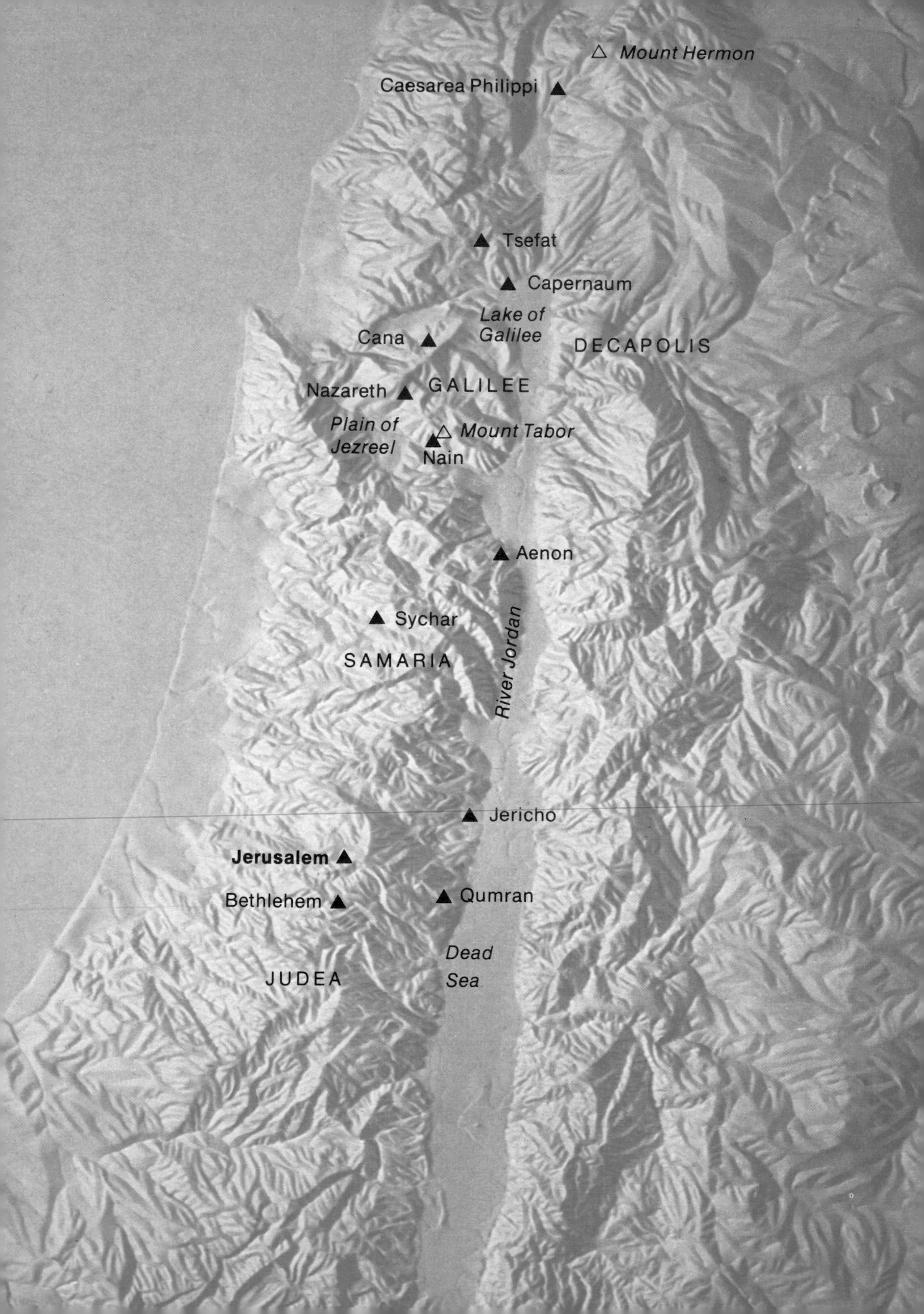

△ *Mount Hermon*

Caesarea Philippi ▲

▲ Tsefat

▲ Capernaum

Lake of Galilee

Cana ▲

DECAPOLIS

Nazareth ▲ GALILEE

Plain of Jezreel △ *Mount Tabor*

▲ Nain

▲ Aenon

▲ Sychar

River Jordan

SAMARIA

▲ Jericho

Jerusalem ▲

Bethlehem ▲   ▲ Qumran

Dead Sea

JUDEA

Part Two

The New Testament

Introduction

Those who have been to the sites of the New Testament story, in Israel and Jordan, Greece and Turkey, will know the excitement of seeing the places where the events actually took place. It makes the Bible events come to life. It helps us understand the text of the New Testament afresh. The aim of this book is the same; to provide pictures which make the setting of the New Testament live for those who cannot visit the places themselves.

It often comes as a surprise to the visitor to the Middle East to find so many remains from New Testament Times. There is no reason why there should be this surprise, for the Bible consists of documents which are at least as trustworthy historically as any ancient writings. But each year sees some new attack on the Bible's reliability (usually by people who do not want it to be true because they do not dare to face the challenge of its message). So it still comes as a confirmation to faith when people find its setting so obviously and accurately that of the Jewish, Roman and Hellenistic world which has left so many traces for us to see and admire.

In fact the person looking for New Testament sites often finds himself on the main tourist track. Places such as Ephesus in Western Turkey not only provide a marvellous aid to under-standing the drama of the New Testament Acts and Epistles but are also among the main attractions of the area for those who have no prior interest in the Bible. This serves to underline the fact that the events of the New Testament which so determined the subsequent history, culture and hope of the civilized world took place at a unique time in history. Hebrew religion, Greek language and culture, Roman imperial administration made possible the immediate and widespread dissemination of the Christian good news. No wonder Paul maintained that 'the time had fully come'. The time was ripe in a way which

it has never been before or since.

The choice of pictures has been determined by the aim of the book. Thus some of the traditional sites have not been included, although they have been hallowed by centuries of devotion, because they no longer help us to imagine what it must have been like in New Testament times. The picture of a first-century tomb complete with rolling stone is quite simply more informative and more evocative than a picture of the church built on the traditional site of Jesus' burial. A photograph of the Roman pavement where Jesus actually stood trial before Pilate has been chosen as more suitable for this particular purpose than, say, one which shows the Stations of the Cross.

The aim of this book, then, is not only simple; it is practical. It is intended to help ordinary people understand the Bible all the better for seeing it against its background, and to remind them that it is not a fairy story to be grown out of, but the record of what actually happened over nineteen hundred years ago in Mediterranean towns and countryside which can still be seen.

The Bible is historical. But it is more than that. It is meant to take us beyond the background, which can be conjured up with the help of a book such as this, to the Person who is at the centre of the picture. He has not changed. He is alive today, and as relevant as when the message of his forgiveness, power and challenge revolutionized the ancient world. It is hoped that the stimulus of these photographs and brief accompanying comment will make many turn afresh to read the New Testament itself with a new confidence in its historicity and a new willingness to hear its message.

Michael Green
St Aldate's
Oxford

Bethlehem stands on a ridge on the edge of the arid Judean desert, 5 miles/8km south-west of Jerusalem.

Up the steep escarpment from the broad Plain of Jezreel, Nazareth lies cupped in the hills of Galilee, 1230ft/ 375m above sea level.
In the Old Testament Nazareth is not mentioned at all, but by Jesus' time it was a busy town near the crossroads of Roman trade-routes. Today it is a sizeable community.

5
THE LIFE AND TEACHING OF JESUS

Bethlehem

'In those days Caesar Augustus issued a decree that a census should be taken of the entire Roman world . . . So Joseph also went up from the town of Nazareth in Galilee to Judea, to Bethlehem the town of David, because he belonged to the house and line of David. He went there to register with Mary, who was pledged to be married to him and was expecting a child. While they were there, the time came for the baby to be born, and she gave birth to her firstborn, a son.' Luke 2:1–7

On the steep hillsides around the town, shepherds still watch their flocks, as they did on the momentous night when Jesus, the Son of God, was born.

In those days, the province of Judea was under Roman occupation. The Emperor's census was a means of assessing the province for tax. It was on his orders that Mary and Joseph set out on their long journey. Yet his decree served God's purpose. For God had said, through the prophet Micah, that a ruler would come from Bethlehem 'who will govern my people Israel'.

Nazareth

Although Jesus was born in Bethlehem, Nazareth was very much his home-town. His parents brought him back there after all the events that followed his birth.

'Joseph and Mary . . . returned to Galilee to their own town of Nazareth. And the child grew and became strong; he was filled with wisdom, and the grace of God was upon him.' Luke 2:39, 40

Here Joseph worked as a carpenter, and Jesus followed in his footsteps. The major part of Jesus' life was spent in this small town, where he grew up through childhood into an adult life as an ordinary tradesman. And yet it was these growing years that earned him 'favour with God and men'. It was about this working life that the voice from heaven said at his baptism 'I am pleased with you'. The years spent at Nazareth show us the rich possibilities of an everyday life lived as God wants it.

Aenon near Salim

'John was baptising at Aenon near Salim, because there was plenty of water, and people were constantly coming to be baptised.' John 3:23

John the Baptist called people to turn from evil because 'the Kingdom of God was near'. He urged them to shed their sin like dead leaves, and to undergo the public 'washing' of baptism, as a sign that God forgave them. His message was stern and uncompromising.

John saw himself fulfilling the task predicted by the prophets for the one who would prepare the way for God's promised Messiah. Certainly his preaching would have created a climate of religious ferment in the region, and this background made people the more ready for the public ministry of Jesus which followed directly after.

In a country where water is scarce, it was natural that John's activity should be concentrated in the area round the Jordan river. The Jordan runs through a deep rift valley, much of it well below sea level. The heat and humidity produce sub-tropical vegetation. The crowds who streamed out to hear John preach and be baptized by him came largely from the area round Jerusalem. They were undertaking a hard journey, across hill-country and down into the valley. This indicates that his impact on the society of his day was very considerable.

He was always eager to deflect attention from himself to 'the man who will come after me'. This greater one would be so superior that John felt unworthy to do him the smallest service. In particular, the coming Messiah's ministry would be greater than John's because he would 'baptize with the Holy Spirit'. John was the last Old Testament-style prophet. When Jesus took over from him the new era had arrived. The life-changing power of God's Spirit was made available for everyone ready to repent. John's true greatness is seen in his willingness to stand down when the time was right for Jesus to begin his own ministry.

River Jordan

'Then Jesus came from Galilee to the Jordan to be baptised by John. But John tried to deter him, saying, "I need to be baptised by you, and do you come to me?" Jesus replied, "Let it be so now; it is proper for us to do this to fulfil all righteousness."'
Matthew 3:13–15

John found it surprising that Jesus should come to him for baptism. After all, the crowds were baptized as a sign of God's cleansing from sin, and he had committed none. But Jesus wanted to identify himself with the sins of his people. His baptism also marked the beginning of his life as a wandering teacher. He would never go back to his settled existence as a carpenter at Nazareth. When he heard a voice from heaven and saw the Holy Spirit come down and rest on him, it was clear evidence that he had been appointed God's servant. And the words he heard declared him to be something more than that: 'This is my own dear Son.'

The Jordan river rises at the foot of Mount Hermon on the border with Lebanon and Syria. South of Lake Galilee it winds down through dense shrubs and thickets towards the Dead Sea. The distance between the mountain rims on each side of the valley is 9–12 miles/15–20km. No major road follows the valley because of the broken and difficult ground created by the Jordan and its tributaries.

The Judean Desert

'Then Jesus was led by the Spirit into the desert to be tempted by the devil. After fasting forty days and forty nights, he was hungry. The tempter came to him and said, "If you are the Son of God, tell these stones to become bread."'
Matthew 4:1–3

Jesus moved straight from the waters of the Jordan to this arid, stony desert south of Jerusalem. Here he faced in advance the temptations that would threaten his whole ministry. His answer to the tempter is in words which go back to the testing of Israel in the wilderness centuries before, 'Man cannot live on bread alone . . .'

'Then the devil took Jesus to the holy city and made him stand on the highest point of the temple . . .' The great south-east corner of the temple area was the vivid setting for Jesus' next temptation. 'If you are the Son of God, throw yourself down . . .' (Matthew 4:5, 6)

Galilee fishing-boats

Jesus went back from the Judean desert to his home territory of Galilee. Here began his brief years as a teacher and healer. Soon he started to call together a small band of men – later called 'the apostles'.

'As Jesus walked beside the Sea of Galilee, he saw Simon and his brother Andrew casting a net into the lake, for they were fishermen. "Come, follow me," Jesus said, "and I will make you fishers of men." At once they left their nets and followed him. When he had gone a little farther, he saw James son of Zebedee and his brother John in a boat, preparing their nets. Without delay he called them . . .' Mark 1:16–20

These first followers were fishermen, and Jesus uses their trade as a picture of what they will later become. In the years after their Master's death and resurrection, they were to draw together a great company of people – the beginnings of the worldwide Christian church. But first they must undergo intensive training, travelling with Jesus, watching him draw people to himself, and discussing with him the meaning of everything he did.

The Galilee fishing industry was a sizeable one in New Testament times. The fish was dried and taken to Jerusalem (via the 'Fish Gate'). John's detailed knowledge of Jerusalem suggests that the family business may have had a 'city office' there. A reference in Pliny to the fish pickled at Tarichaea by Galilee shows that it was exported throughout the Mediterranean world.

Cana in Galilee

'A wedding took place at Cana in Galilee. Jesus' mother was there, and Jesus and his disciples had also been invited to the wedding . . .' John 2:1, 2

John's Gospel is constructed round seven miracles. He calls them 'signs': each of them points to an aspect of the meaning of the coming of Jesus. The first he selects took place at a wedding in Cana of Galilee. When the wine for the feast ran short, Jesus turned water into wine. The water was for 'the Jewish rites of purification' – the detailed rules for washing household utensils. Jesus had come to bring an entirely new way of life and religion: the wine of the new age, the gospel.

The village lies among the Galilean hills. It was the home of one of the apostles, Nathanael. It was also the site of one of Jesus' few 'miracles at a distance', when he healed the son of an official from Capernaum.

The name 'Cana' is preserved in the present-day village of Kafr Kana, a few miles east of Nazareth. Villagers still come to the well in Kafr Kana to draw water.

Capernaum

'They went to Capernaum, and when the Sabbath came, Jesus went into the synagogue and began to teach. The people were amazed at his teaching, because he taught them as one who had authority, not as the teachers of the law.' Mark 1:21, 22

Capernaum, on the north-west shore of Lake Galilee, was Jesus' base for much of his teaching and healing ministry. It was the home of Peter and Andrew, and here Jesus healed Peter's mother-in-law.

It was also in Capernaum that a paralyzed man was carried to Jesus by four friends. Finding the crowds too dense to penetrate, they forced a hole in the roof and lowered him to where Jesus was.

There was a tax-collecting station in the village, and Jesus called one of its officials, Levi (Matthew), to follow him. This caused a lot of local opposition. Despite all that happened there, the people of the town did not believe Jesus' message, and he had to warn them of coming judgement.

The palm, carved on the synagogue stonework, was a symbol of the land of Israel.

The synagogue at Capernaum in Jesus' time had been built by the Roman centurion whose slave was healed by Jesus. The ruin of the synagogue on the site of Capernaum today dates from a hundred years or so later, but it shows the same combination of Roman architecture and Jewish symbolism that would have characterized the earlier one. Such buildings must have reminded the people constantly that, although their religion was still Jewish, all the power belonged to the occupying Romans.

More Jewish symbols: a bunch of grapes and a star.

Galilee countryside

'Jesus travelled about from one town and village to another, proclaiming the good news of the kingdom of God. The Twelve were with him . . .'
Luke 8:1

Behind the hills which flank the edge of the plain of Jezreel lies Nazareth. The village in the foreground is at the foot of Mount Tabor. In New Testament times Galilee was at the intersection of important trade-routes: Jesus' teaching was in no backwater but in a busy, if second-class, province of the Roman Empire. As well as preaching in these villages himself, Jesus sent out seventy of his disciples to prepare the way for him. He told them the inhabitants were like a harvest ready to be reaped.

Known as the 'Mount of Precipitation' this rocky hill is near Nazareth. It might well have been where Jesus was taken when the outraged inhabitants of Nazareth threatened to 'throw him down headlong'. The claims of Jesus were too much for the people of his own home town. 'A prophet is not without honour, except in his own country.'

City on a hill

'A city on a hill cannot be hidden. Neither do people light a lamp and put it under a bowl. Instead they put it on its stand, and it gives light to everyone in the house. In the same way, let your light shine before men, that they may see your good deeds and praise your Father in heaven.'
Matthew 5:14–16

Much of the teaching of Jesus was in the form of object-lessons and parables from life around. This is one of the reasons he held such appeal for the ordinary local people.

The 'city on a hill' pictured here is Tsefat in Upper Galilee, for long a centre of Jewish learning and devotion.

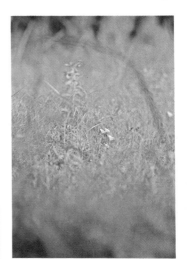

Oil lamps typical of the very many found from Roman and later periods (Archaeological Museum, Istanbul). To put them under a covering is not only to hide their light but also to ensure they go out, for lack of oxygen.

'Beware of practising your piety before men.' Matthew 6:1

The central part of Jesus'˙ Sermon on the Mount is about hypocrisy: concern with outward piety and not real 'heart' religion.

'Consider the lilies of the field, how they grow . . .' Matthew 6:28

In these famous words Jesus pointed to an uncomplicated faith in God who cares for plants and animals, as the antidote to worry and stress.

Jacob's well

'Jesus came to a town in Samaria called Sychar, near the plot of ground Jacob had given to his son Joseph. Jacob's well was there, and Jesus, tired as he was from the journey, sat down by the well . . . A Samaritan woman came to draw water . . .'
John 4:5–7

Not only racial prejudice but also the low view Jews held of women made it surprising that Jesus stopped to talk to the woman at the well. But the result was a vital conversation. He showed his insight into deep secrets of personal life, and an understanding compassion towards moral failure. He also spoke of himself as the answer to our longing for fulfilment: 'Whoever drinks the water I give him will never thirst. Indeed, the water I give him will become in him a spring of water welling up to eternal life.'

The well on the facing page is typical of those still in use in country areas. Jesus had chosen to take the direct route from Judea to Galilee, passing through Samaria. Most Jews would have made a wide detour, because they hated the Samaritans. They looked upon them as half-castes, and despised their centre of worship on Mount Gerizim.

Jacob's well itself is now enclosed within a church; it is still true that 'the well is deep'; and the water is as good as when Jacob first dug it.

The Good Shepherd

'The sheep listen to his voice. He calls his own sheep by name and leads them out . . . he goes on ahead of them, and his sheep follow him because they know his voice . . . I am the good shepherd; I know my sheep and my sheep know me . . . and I lay down my life for the sheep.' John 10:3, 4, 14

Jesus' lovely word-picture of the shepherd is the nearest we find to a parable in John's Gospel. It points to the kind of relationship Jesus has with his followers: one of total trust on their part and total trustworthiness on his. He understands what they need, and they learn to distinguish his voice from all others.

But still Jesus warns them against heeding anyone else who might call them to follow. He uses the picture of the hired hand, who can never have the same level of commitment to the sheep as the shepherd himself.

In contrast, Jesus tells them that his care for them will not stop short of death. What this sacrifice means he gives no clue here, but it is one of several times when he teaches them about the positive value of the death he knows he will die.

Finally he takes the point of the illustration one stage further when he speaks of 'other sheep who are not of this fold. I must bring them also.' The followers of Jesus during his lifetime were almost all Jews. But within a few years of his death and resurrection they were to become an international company.

Nain

'Soon afterwards, Jesus went to a town called Nain, and his disciples and a large crowd went along with him. As he approached the town gate, a dead person was being carried out – the only son of his mother, and she was a widow . . . When the Lord saw her, his heart went out to her . . .'
Luke 7:11–13

This young man at Nain; Jairus' daughter at Capernaum; Lazarus at Bethany – the occasions when Jesus raised people from the dead were few, but deeply significant. Each time he was moved by pity for the bereaved: to be a childless widow in the culture of the day would have condemned the mother to shame as well as loneliness. But these miracles point to

Nain, a village on the slope of a hill looking towards the rounded hump of Mount Tabor, was the scene of the demonstration of the power of Jesus over death itself.

something more than simply Jesus' compassion. They foreshadow his own resurrection by showing his supremacy over death. The life he gives cannot be quenched even by the grave.

Storm over the lake

Jesus claimed power not only over sickness and death itself, but also over creation.

'Leaving the crowd behind, they took him along, just as he was, in the boat. There were also other boats with him. A furious squall came up, and the waves broke over the boat . . . He got up, rebuked the wind and said to the waves, "Quiet! Be still!"' Mark 4:36–39

Fishing boats used on Lake Galilee are small, and a storm can soon blot out the coast-line and raise a heavy sea. When Jesus calmed the storm, his disciples saw it as one more piece of evidence that they were in the presence of someone greater than they could adequately explain. 'Who then is this? Even the wind and the waves obey him!'

Lake Galilee

'Jesus made the disciples get in the boat and go on ahead of him to the other side, while he dismissed the crowd.' Matthew 14:22

Jesus used the lake as an escape route from the crowds. He borrowed a boat from the fishermen who became his followers, and taught the people on the beach from the boat. Later, the lake was used to teach his disciples faith. They were rowing across it at night when he came to them, walking on the water.

This view is of the north-western corner of the lake, looking from near Tiberias towards the site of Magdala and Gennesaret.

The sower

'He told them many things in parables, saying, "A farmer went out to sow his seed. As he was scattering the seed, some fell along the path, and the birds came and ate it up. Some fell on rocky places . . . among thorns . . . on good soil . . ."'
Matthew 13:3–8

Jesus' parables appealed to people's will as much as their understanding. Only people who really wanted to follow him would grasp the meaning. The parable of the sower illustrates this. The seed was the message Jesus brought, and anyone alive to the need to receive it was bound to ask himself how deeply he was taking it in. Was it just a superficial, immediate response? Or would what he heard make a lasting change in his life?

The picture of the 'soils' was taken in Galilee; Mount Moreh is in the background.

The Good Samaritan

'A man was going down from Jerusalem to Jericho, when he fell into the hands of robbers. They stripped him of his clothes, beat him and went away, leaving him half-dead . . .'
Luke 10:30

Jesus' story of the man who was beaten up on the Jericho road would have been only too real to his hearers in Jerusalem. The road passes through rocky, desert country as it winds down to Jericho in the Jordan valley. The ruin of an inn still stands where an inn has stood for centuries. But the twist in the story may not have proved so easy to accept: it was a despised Samaritan, not the religious people, who showed true love for his neighbour. The scribe (religious teacher) who had asked 'Who is my neighbour?' was brought to see that he could not pick and choose. Our neighbour is anyone in need.

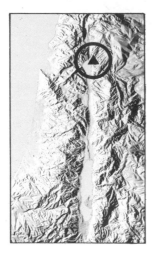

Lakeside miracles

'They went across the lake to the region of the Gerasenes. When Jesus got out of the boat, a man with an evil spirit came from the tombs to meet him . . . The evil spirits came out and went into the pigs. The herd, about two thousand in number, rushed down the steep bank into the lake and were drowned.' Mark 5:1-2, 13

This story is the most remarkable of many in the Gospels where Jesus healed 'demoniacs', people believed to be possessed by evil spirits. The man he found among the tombs was completely transformed.

The district of Gerasa, Gadara and Gergesa was east of the Lake of Galilee, an area known for its 'ten towns', or decapolis, occupied by Greeks: this would explain why there was so large a herd of swine, for pork was a forbidden food for the Jew. The picture looks towards the north-eastern end of the lake.

These fish are known today as 'St Peter's fish' because of their large mouth (in which they carry their eggs); see the story in Matthew 17:27. The fish in the story of the feeding of the five thousand may well, however, have been pickled, or salted, rather than fresh.

It was at the north-east end of the lake, too, that a crowd of five thousand were fed from five loaves and two small fishes. The crowd misunderstood the meaning of the miracle, interpreting it too materialistically. John's Gospel tells how this led Jesus to describe himself as 'the bread of life' – sent to sustain people in a life which would survive death.

Caesarea Philippi

'When Jesus came to the region of Caesarea Philippi, he asked his disciples, "Who do people say the Son of Man is?" . . . Simon Peter answered, "You are the Christ, the Son of the living God." Jesus replied, ". . . you are Peter, and on this rock I will build my church . . ."'
Matthew 16:13, 16–18

It gradually dawns on the disciples that their friend is more than just a great teacher and healer. Then, on a journey to the north of Galilee, Jesus judges the time has come to draw out from them a full declaration of who they understand him to be. Peter makes the confession that has been the central belief of Christians down the centuries. Jesus tells him it has been revealed to him by God.

From this point on, events begin to move towards the final climax of the story in Jerusalem.

Caesarea Philippi was built by the tetrarch Philip (son of Herod the Great) and dedicated to 'Caesar', the Roman Emperor. It was formerly known as Paneas, derived from the veneration of the 'Great God Pan'. So it was against the background both of Emperor worship and 'pantheism' that Peter made his confession; and against the backcloth of a rock cliff which dominates one of the sources of the Jordan.

Mount Hermon

'Jesus took with him Peter, James and John the brother of James, and led them up a high mountain by themselves. There he was transfigured before them. His face shone like the sun, and his clothes became as white as the light.'
Matthew 17:1, 2

Once they had come to realize who he was, Jesus took the inmost circle of his disciples aside. It was time to give them a glimpse of the heavenly dimension from which the Son of God came and to which he would return.

The appearance of Moses and Elijah connects Jesus with the very greatest in Israel's history. But the words of the voice from heaven place him on an altogether different level of being. 'This is my Son, whom I love; with him I am well pleased.'

The transfiguration took place six days after Peter's confession at Caesarea Philippi. Mount Hermon is in the same area, and so it has long been supposed that this mountain was the site of the transfiguration. It is certainly a 'high mountain', rising to 9,100ft/977m, and dominating Upper Galilee. The picture is of dawn over Mount Hermon.

6
OPPOSITION AND TRIUMPH

Synagogue

'He went into the synagogue, and a man with a shrivelled hand was there. Some of them were looking for a reason to accuse Jesus, so they watched him closely to see if he would heal him on the Sabbath.' Mark 3:1, 2

From the beginning of his ministry Jesus taught in the Jewish synagogues. But the religious leaders who had reduced the law to a tyranny of petty rules strongly resented every move he made to restore the true meaning of God's law.

Another synagogue: both are in Tsefat, in Galilee.

An orthodox Jew with a phylactery – passages from the law in a small box – bound to his forehead in literal obedience to commandments such as Deuteronomy 6:8. They are worn both on the head and on the left hand.

The clash with orthodoxy

'Then some Pharisees and teachers of the law came to Jesus from Jerusalem and asked, "Why do your disciples break the tradition of the elders? They don't wash their hands before they eat!" Jesus replied, "And why do you break the command of God for the sake of your tradition? . . ."'
Matthew 15:1–3

In such places as Tsefat, pictured here, and the Mea Shearim quarter of Jerusalem today, ultra-orthodox Jews seek to live out the minutiae of the observance of the law and rabbinic traditions. Jesus taught that the life of the new age of the gospel was so different from the old that the traditional structures could not hold it. New wine needed new wineskins. This made a clash with the upholders of orthodoxy inevitable.

Those who led 'little ones' astray were fit only to have a millstone tied round their necks and be cast into the sea.

Jesus compared the Pharisees to 'whited sepulchres', tombs whitewashed outside but rotten inside. He insisted that no amount of religious observance, however detailed, could make up for a heart not right with God.

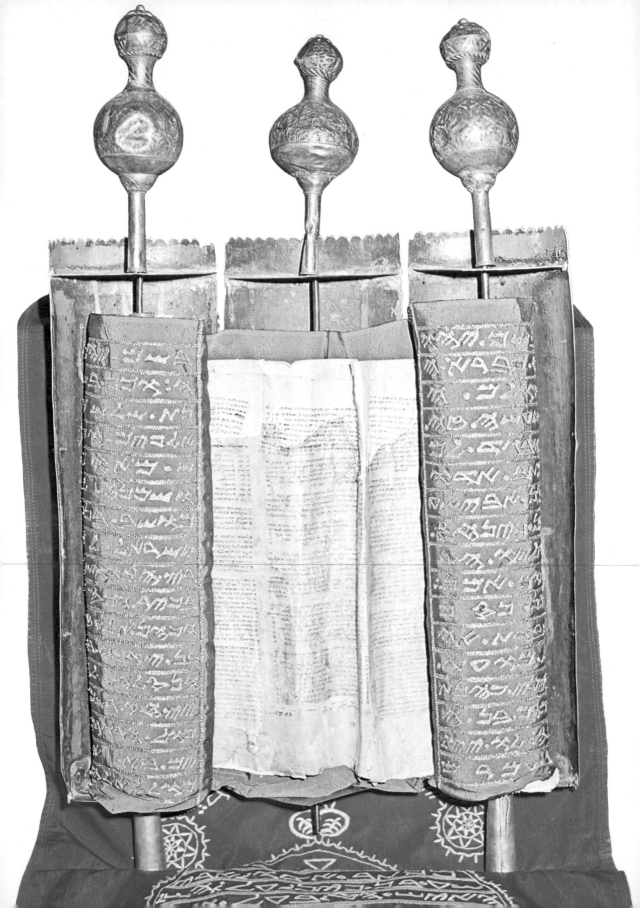

The law

'Do not think that I have come to abolish the Law or the Prophets; I have not come to abolish them but to fulfil them. I tell you the truth, until heaven and earth disappear, not the smallest letter, not the least stroke of a pen, will by any means disappear from the Law until everything is accomplished.' Matthew 5:17, 18

Jesus set a very high value on the Old Testament; for him, as for his fellow Jews, God spoke through its writings. But he had come to 'fulfil' Old Testament teaching. Only now that he had come could 'the Law and Prophets' be understood in their full meaning.

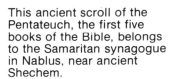

This ancient scroll of the Pentateuch, the first five books of the Bible, belongs to the Samaritan synagogue in Nablus, near ancient Shechem.

An orthodox Jew studying the law.

Jerusalem

'As Jesus approached Jerusalem and saw the city, he wept over it and said, "If you, even you, had only known on this day what would bring you peace – but now it is hidden from your eyes. The days will come upon you when your enemies will build an embankment against you and encircle you and hem you in on every side . . . "'
Luke 19:41–44

The Old City of Jerusalem is enclosed by walls dating back to medieval times. It is a square-shaped maze of narrow streets and ancient buildings. The more modern buildings of the new Jerusalem rise behind. It would have been an impressive sight as Jesus approached the city before his triumphal entry on Palm Sunday, but his first reaction is of grief that this centre of Jewish religion did not understand what God was doing.

The Pool of Bethesda

'Now there is in Jerusalem near the Sheep Gate a pool, which in Aramaic is called Bethesda . . . Here a great number of disabled people used to lie – the blind, the lame, the paralysed. One who was there had been an invalid for thirty-eight years . . . Jesus said to him, "Get up! Pick up your mat and walk." ' John 5:2-5, 8

John's Gospel records only two straightforward healings, both of them at pools in Jerusalem. These pools seem to have been considered places of healing. In both John's healing stories, Bethesda and Siloam, the men Jesus healed were at first unaware of who he was. They only came to believe in him when he sought them out personally and spoke with them. Both acts of mercy were performed on the sabbath, which led to conflict with the religious leaders.

Archaeologists discovered, deep below the present level of Jerusalem, a pool with five covered colonnades . . . Mixed with remains from Crusader times there is stonework going back to the time of Jesus himself, and earlier.

The pool of Siloam goes back to the engineering feat of Hezekiah about 700 BC, when a rock tunnel 1,700ft/ 517m long was dug to bring water inside the city from a spring outside.

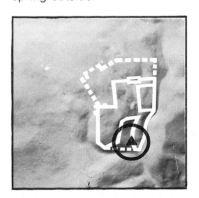

At Bethesda that was relatively minor but at Siloam the controversy was prolonged and bitter. The man healed of congenital blindness (his story is told in John 9) puts up a spirited defence, both of himself and of Jesus. His case is unanswerable: 'Whether this man is a sinner or not, I don't know. One thing I do know: I was blind but now I see!'

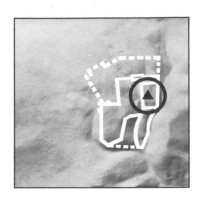

The temple area

'In the temple courts Jesus found men selling cattle, sheep and doves, and others sitting at tables exchanging money. So he made a whip out of cords, and drove all from the temple area, both sheep and cattle; he scattered the coins of the money changers and overturned their tables. To those who sold doves he said, "Get these out of here! How dare you turn my Father's house into a market!"'
John 2:13–16

In the temple there was a ceaseless round of sacrifices, as ordinary people brought animals of all kinds to be sacrificed by the priests according to the instructions in the law of Moses. Many would purchase the beasts from merchants trading within the temple area. There were also specialized bankers who converted the common coinage into the currency used in the temple, making a profit on each transaction.

The contradiction of this profiteering from the poor alongside the worship of God moved Jesus to deep anger. This brought his conflict with established religion right into the temple.

The large temple area, formerly resplendent with courts and colonnades, is now almost bare except for two large mosques. The golden-domed Mosque of Omar stands over the rock of Mount Moriah, where Abraham showed his willingness to sacrifice his son Isaac. Solomon's original temple was looted and destroyed at the time when Jerusalem fell to Nebuchadnezzar of Babylon. When the exiles returned, they eventually rebuilt on the same site. This second temple stood for several centuries, but was itself virtually replaced by Herod's temple, which was almost complete by Jesus' time. In AD 70 it was sacked by the Romans after the long siege of Jerusalem. It has never been rebuilt.

Teachers would gather their disciples round them in the temple colonnades. Here too the early Christians met. 'All the believers used to meet together in Solomon's colonnade' (Acts 5:12).

Inscription in Greek forbidding Gentiles on pain of death to enter the Temple precincts (see Acts 21:28) (Istanbul Archaeological Museum).

The future

'When you see Jerusalem surrounded by armies, you will know that its desolation is near. Then let those who are in Judea flee to the mountains, let those in the city get out, and let those in the country not enter the city . . .' Luke 21:20, 21

Towards the end of his ministry, Jesus taught about what would happen in years to come. He spoke of the end of time, of his own return as Lord of the universe. But interwoven with all this were predictions of what would happen to Jerusalem in the much nearer future – destruction and great suffering.

The city was indeed besieged and then sacked by the Romans forty years later in AD 70. It has never been rebuilt. The survival of Judaism since that time has depended on the synagogues.

In a relief on the Titus Arch in Rome, plunder from the temple at Jerusalem is seen being carried in triumph by the victorious Romans. The seven-branched lampstand was one of the basic pieces of furniture, first in the desert tabernacle and then in the temple.

In 1947 the Dead Sea Scrolls, largely manuscripts of Old Testament books, were discovered in a cave by a shepherd boy. They had lain untouched since being hidden there before the Roman army overran the area in AD 68. Nearby are the remains of Qumran, the settlement of the Jewish monastic community which owned the manuscripts. There are clear evidences of violent destruction in the ruins.

Jerusalem street

'When it was almost time for the Jewish Passover, many went up from the country to Jerusalem . . . They kept looking for Jesus . . . "What do you think? Isn't he coming to the Feast at all?" But the chief priests and Pharisees had given orders that if anyone found out where Jesus was, he should report it so that they might arrest him.'
John 11:55–57

When Jesus arrived in Jerusalem a week before his death, it was crowded with pilgrims up for the Passover Festival. The city was full of debate, rumour and intrigue about him. The conflict with the religious leaders, slowly building for months, was now coming to a head. The furore caused by the raising of Lazarus at Bethany had finally convinced the authorities that they must deal with Jesus before their influence dwindled. Jerusalem, the centre of Jewish religious devotion, was the only possible stage for such a confrontation. 'One man must die for the people,' said Caiaphas, the high priest.

In the tangle of narrow streets in the old city of Jerusalem, it is easy to imagine the rapidly-spreading rumour and counter-rumour as tension built up around Jesus.

The village of Bethany, about 2 miles/3km from Jerusalem, offered Jesus a refuge away from the crowded city. Probably he returned there each night during his last week. It was the home of his close friends, Martha, Mary and Lazarus – and the scene of the most striking of all Jesus' miracles (John 11).

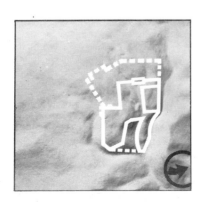

The vine

'I am the vine; you are the branches. If a man remains in me and I in him, he will bear much fruit; apart from me you can do nothing. If anyone does not remain in me, he is like a branch that is thrown away and withers . . . This is to my Father's glory, that you bear much fruit, showing yourselves to be my disciples.'
John 15:5, 6, 8

At the Last Supper, in the upper room the night before his death, Jesus taught his disciples many things that would strengthen them in the time after he had gone. His teaching included the last of his great 'I am' sayings – 'I am the true vine'. The seven 'I am' sayings use everyday things – bread, light, shepherd, door, life, way, vine – to picture the believer's relationship to Jesus.

Each branch of a vine grows directly from the main 'stock'. After the grapes are picked the branches are cut right back, nearly to the stock. For much of the year the stock grows round them – they 'remain', or 'abide', in the vine. Then the new branches grow out rapidly to bear fruit. Branches which do not bear fruit are cut off altogether: they are of no use for anything but to be burnt.

The picture makes it vividly clear that Jesus does not think it possible for people to live up to his standards by their own efforts. The 'good fruit' comes as they draw their life from him – 'apart from me you can do nothing.'

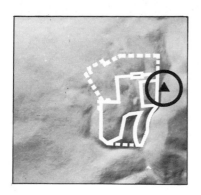

Gethsemane

'When he had finished praying, Jesus left with his disciples and crossed the Kidron Valley. On the other side there was an olive grove, and he and his disciples went into it.' John 18:1

Down from the walls of the old city, across a small valley, and up the slopes of the Mount of Olives opposite, there was a secluded garden where, John tells us, Jesus often met with his disciples. In the Garden of Gethsemane the tortured forms of the ancient olive trees, centuries old, still recall the agony Jesus went through before his final arrest.

In his real humanity, he is appalled by the prospect of what he will be called on to undergo the next day. He knows how overwhelming the horror of his death will be: not just the physical pain of crucifixion, but the spiritual burden of the evil and alienation which come from human sin – the blackness of separation from his Father.

In his anguish he prays to be spared the cross. But finally he comes to the point of accepting what is necessary if humanity is to be redeemed: 'not as I will, but as you will.'

He calls his closest disciples to share with him in prayer, but they are unable to stay awake – the first of several failures to stand with him in his time of great need. Jesus is spiritually alone.

Judas knows that the garden is their frequent place of meeting, and he leads the guards there as his act of betrayal, which is made still more insidious by the famous 'kiss' by which he identifies Jesus to the guards.

The actual 'Pavement' of the Roman Fort of Antonia (the praetorium) was recently discovered under the Sisters of Zion Convent in Jerusalem. Scratched on some of the paving stones are the games the Roman soldiers once played. (This one is said to be for the ancient 'game of a king'. Traditionally the loser lost his life – it was a game often played with condemned prisoners. Kings would play it themselves – and if they lost have a slave put to death on their behalf.)

The Pavement

'Then the Jews led Jesus from Caiaphas to the palace of the Roman governor . . . Pilate tried to set Jesus free, but the Jews kept shouting, "If you let this man go, you are no friend of Caesar. Anyone who claims to be a king opposes Caesar."

'When Pilate heard this, he brought Jesus out and sat down on the judge's seat at a place known as The Stone Pavement (which in Aramaic is Gabbatha) . . . "Here is your king," Pilate said to the Jews. But they shouted, "Take him away! Take him away! Crucify him!"' John 18:28; 19:12–15

Jesus underwent at least two 'trials'. The first was a Jewish one, conducted before the high priest and (perhaps later) the whole council (Sanhedrin). The main thrust of the accusation was blasphemy, but the trial was made ineffective by the failure of witnesses to agree.

The Jewish leaders then passed Jesus on to the Roman governor, Pilate, on the grounds that they had no authority to execute him. They could have put him to death by stoning, as they did Stephen. What they could not do was crucify him, and nothing less than this would satisfy them, as the Roman authorities had to be implicated in his death.

The charge in this Roman trial shifted subtly to one of making himself out to be a king. But Pilate was not fooled, and tried several times to avoid the necessity of putting Jesus to death. In the end, though, expediency triumphed over justice, and the death was decreed that Jesus had always foretold, and which proved to be the fulfilment of Old Testament prophecies.

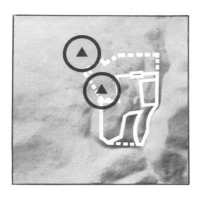

It is not certain precisely where Jesus was crucified. Traditionally it was on the site now marked by the Church of the Holy Sepulchre, which was formerly outside the city walls. Research on the location of the walls in New Testament times continues. It was General Gordon in the last century who suggested that this rocky outcrop outside the present northern wall bore a striking resemblance to the shape of a skull.

Place of a skull

'They brought Jesus to the place called Golgotha (which means The Place of the Skull). Then they offered him wine mixed with myrrh, but he did not take it. And they crucified him. Dividing up his clothes, they cast lots to see what each would get. It was the third hour when they crucified him . . .'
Mark 15:22–24

A remarkably high proportion of what is written in the Gospels (at least a third) is connected with the last week of Jesus' life, and particularly his death. Why is so much importance given to what in most biographies takes up just part of the last chapter?

The teaching of the rest of the New Testament makes the reason clear. The mission of Jesus was not simply to teach about God and about the life he wants us to live. It was also to rescue humanity – from a predicament we do not always realize we are in.

The New Testament writers use several metaphors to explain what Jesus' death achieved. It was a deliverance – from captivity to sin into the freedom of a new relationship with God; a redemption – a price paid to buy us back from slavery into sonship; a way of reconciliation – by which our alienation from God is exchanged for friendship with him. In the language of the law-court, Paul explains it as a means of 'justification', through which we who are guilty before God can be forgiven and acquitted. In Paul's great words: 'God made him who had no sin to be sin for us, so that in him we might become the righteousness of God.'

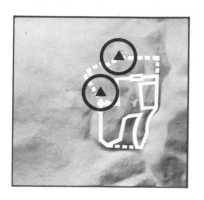

The empty tomb

'When the Sabbath was over, Mary Magdalene, Mary the mother of James, and Salome bought spices so that they might go to anoint Jesus' body. Very early on the first day of the week, just after sunrise, they were on their way to the tomb and they asked each other, "Who will roll the stone away from the entrance of the tomb?"

'But when they looked up, they saw that the stone, which was very large, had been rolled away . . .' Mark 16:1–4

In an ancient garden near 'Gordon's Calvary' outside the walls of Jerusalem is this tomb, a vivid example of the type in which Jesus was laid. A groove in the rock took the great stone which was rolled in front of the entrance. The women had been forced to delay anointing Jesus' body because of the sabbath. The last thing they expected was for Jesus to be raised from death, despite the predictions he had made in his teaching.

Looking out from inside another first-century tomb, the stone in place by the entrance. This one was recently discovered in Nazareth beneath the Convent of the Sisters of Nazareth.

Inside, the body was 'wrapped, with the spices, in strips of linen' (John 19:40). When Peter came to the tomb of Jesus, 'he saw the strips of linen lying there, as well as the burial cloth that had been around Jesus' head. The cloth was folded up by itself, separate from the linen' (John 20:6–7). The body had gone, but the cloths had been left intact.

Looking towards the peaks of Mount Hermon in Upper Galilee.

The great commission

'Then the eleven disciples went to Galilee, to the mountain where Jesus had told them to go. When they saw him, they worshipped him; but some doubted. Then Jesus came to them and said, "All authority in heaven and on earth has been given to me. Therefore go and make disciples of all nations . . ."' Matthew 28:16–19

After his resurrection, Jesus appeared quite frequently, both to individuals and to groups of his disciples. Some of these appearances were in Jerusalem, some in Galilee.

The shore of Lake Galilee.

One took place on the shore of the Lake of Galilee, where the disciples had returned to their fishing. Jesus had prepared a fire on the beach and shared a breakfast of fish and bread with his disciples.

It was a meeting of particular significance for Peter. He had denied Jesus three times during the night of the trial, and must still have felt bitterly disappointed with himself. But Jesus now asked him three times whether he loved him. It was an opportunity for Peter to re-affirm his devotion. Each time Jesus said, 'Feed my sheep'.

213

Ascension

' "You will receive power when the Holy Spirit comes on you; and you will be my witnesses in Jerusalem, and in all Judea and Samaria, and to the ends of the earth." After he said this, he was taken up before their very eyes, and a cloud hid him from their sight.' Acts 1:8, 9

The resurrection appearances of Jesus continued over a period of forty days. They ceased from the time of his ascension, when the disciples were made vividly aware that the time of his presence on earth had ended and he was taking up again his heavenly glory. The way this return to heaven is expressed elsewhere in the New Testament (and in the Christian creeds) is as 'sitting down at the right hand of God'. It is an image of kingship and authority.

The Mount of Olives, where Luke tells us the ascension took place, is a hill overlooking Jerusalem across the Kidron Valley. The tower is of a church built to commemorate the event.

There are two further implications of the ascension, both of them very reassuring to the disciples. One is that Christ has taken the experience of human life right into the presence of God. The other is that, as fully man as well as fully God, he can be an effective mediator between God and men. The bodily ascension of Jesus brought these things home to the disciples in a way that could be felt and seen.

Immediately after the ascension the disciples were given the promise that Jesus would one day return to earth – a promise he had himself frequently given in his teaching. 'This same Jesus, who has been taken from you into heaven, will come back in the same way . . .'

The medieval Damascus Gate in Jerusalem was the starting-point of the trade-route to Damascus in Syria. In New Testament times, as now, Jerusalem was a cosmopolitan city with trade and religious links throughout the ancient world.

7
OUTREACH AND THE EARLY CHURCH

Pentecost

'When the day of Pentecost came, they were all together in one place. Suddenly a sound like the blowing of a violent wind came from heaven and filled the whole house where they were sitting . . . All of them were filled with the Holy Spirit and began to speak in other tongues . . . Now there were staying in Jerusalem God-fearing Jews from every nation under heaven. When they heard this sound, a crowd came together in bewilderment, because each one heard them speaking in his own language.' Acts 2:1–6

Pentecost was a popular Jewish festival, so Jews and 'God-fearers', other nationals interested in Judaism, had gathered in Jerusalem from all round the Mediterranean world. Jesus had promised his disciples would receive power when the Holy Spirit was given them, and Peter's address to the amazed crowd was powerful and closely-reasoned – quite unlike the Peter of the Gospels.

From this time onwards the disciples had power and inspiration to spread the gospel of Jesus, and the Acts of the Apostles is the story of how the good news was taken, from Jerusalem to Judea to Samaria, and outwards until it reached Rome.

Persecution and outreach

'They dragged Stephen out of the city and began to stone him . . . And Saul was there . . . On that day a great persecution broke out against the church at Jerusalem, and all except the apostles were scattered throughout Judea and Samaria. Godly men buried Stephen and mourned deeply for him . . .' Acts 7:58; 8:1, 2

Stephen was the first martyr of the new faith. His death triggered off fresh persecution, and this was to be a feature of the spread of the gospel. But the immediate effect was to take the news about Jesus to a wider area than Jerusalem, as the disciples who had to leave the city 'preached the word wherever they went'. There was also another, longer-term effect: the impact of Stephen's death on the mind of a young man named Saul.

Samaria

'When the apostles in Jerusalem heard that Samaria had accepted the word of God, they sent Peter and John to them . . . When they had testified and proclaimed the word of the Lord, Peter and John returned to Jerusalem preaching the gospel in many Samaritan villages.'
Acts 8:14, 25

The hill-country of Samaria, north from Jerusalem, and Judea, south from Jerusalem, were the obvious starting-points for the outreach of the gospel. Orthodox Jews steered clear of the region of Samaria because they despised the Samaritans: they were of mixed race, and held rival sacrifices on Mount Gerizim. But this did not deter the early Christians. Philip the evangelist 'proclaimed the Christ there', and there was a considerable response.

This village is near the ancient capital of Samaria.

The apostles in Jerusalem heard of this and, perhaps because there might have been doubts in some quarters whether Samaritans were welcome in the church, they visited the city and prayed with the new converts. The result was a kind of 'Samaritan Pentecost', with evident signs of the Holy Spirit at work.

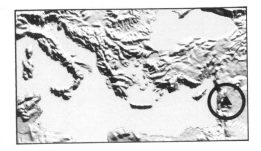

The road to Damascus

'Meanwhile, Saul was still breathing out murderous threats against the Lord's disciples. He went to the high priest and asked him for letters to the synagogues in Damascus, so that if he found any there who belonged to the Way, whether men or women, he might take them as prisoners to Jerusalem. As he neared Damascus on his journey, suddenly a light from heaven flashed around him. He fell to the ground and heard a voice say to him, "Saul, Saul, why do you persecute me?"'
Acts 9:1–4

Saul of Tarsus, who became the apostle Paul, planned to extend his persecution of the church into Damascus. He took the road from the Damascus Gate that passes over the Golan Heights on its way into Syria.
    There the risen Christ spoke unmistakably to him. In persecuting the church he had been persecuting Jesus himself. Saul fell to the ground. When he rose he was blind, and had to be led by the hand into Damascus.

Paul was born in Tarsus, a large Romanized city and university town in what is now south-east Turkey. Pompey and Cicero were two famous Romans who had been involved in its government, and it was visited by Antony. Little remains from Roman times except this arch.

Paul's background equipped him well for the missions to the Gentiles he was later to undertake. A Pharisee who had come to Jerusalem to study under the famous Gamaliel, he was steeped in the Old Testament. But he was also a Roman citizen, which was to prove decisive in later events.

The Street called Straight

'In Damascus there was a disciple named Ananias. The Lord called to him in a vision . . . "Go to the house of Judas on Straight Street and ask for a man from Tarsus named Saul, for he is praying. In a vision he has seen a man named Ananias come and place his hands on him to restore his sight."' Acts 9:10–12

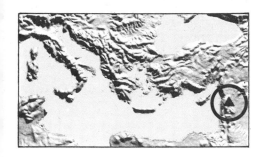

The Street called Straight still exists in Damascus today. It is a busy artery of the old covered markets. A Roman gateway at one end and ancient walls show what was once the extent of the city.

When Saul reached Damascus he was a shattered man. 'For three days he was blind, and did not eat or drink anything.' It must have taken considerable courage for Ananias to obey the vision and visit the arch-persecutor, but when he arrived, Saul's identification with his new Lord's death and resurrection were sealed. His old life had died with Christ. Now he was 'raised again in newness of life'. He was 'in Christ', a 'new creature'. Ananias baptized him, and so began a Christian life and ministry which influenced the scale and shape of Christianity more than any other.

As Saul began to teach in the Damascus synagogues about the Messiahship of Jesus, the disciples took time to accept that their enemy had become their friend. The church in Jerusalem was to find the same problem later on. But his ability in debating the meaning of the Old Testament writings soon marked him out as an ally of considerable importance.

Inevitably the synagogue leaders did not take to his activities, and started a campaign against him which was to be echoed repeatedly in the cities and towns Paul visited on his travels. He had to make his escape from the city by night, ignominiously lowered from the walls in a basket. It was a strange departure for the man who had expected to go back to Jerusalem with a party of fettered prisoners.

Joppa

'"Cornelius . . . send men to Joppa to bring back a man named Simon who is called Peter. He is staying with Simon the tanner, whose house is by the sea." . . .Peter went up on the roof to pray. He became hungry and wanted something to eat, and while the meal was being prepared, he fell into a trance . . .' Acts 10:3, 5, 6, 9, 10

The animals Peter saw in his trance, let down in a sheet from heaven, included many that were forbidden food for Jews. And so he was perplexed when a voice told him to 'kill and eat'. But when men from the Roman centurion Cornelius came to the door, the implications became clear. He had no hesitation in going with them. The gospel was not only for Jews, but also for the Gentiles. Peter told this story several times to the Jewish Christians, because it established such a crucial point. If the Christian message had been confined to the Jewish nation, the course of world history would have been totally different.

This flat roof in Jaffa has lattice-work as a shade against the sun. The equivalent at the house of Simon the tanner would have been an awning tied at the corners. In Peter's trance this would have seemed like a 'great sheet let down to earth'.

Antioch

'Barnabas went to Tarsus to look for Saul, and when he found him, he brought him to Antioch. So for a whole year Barnabas and Saul met with the church and taught great numbers of people. The disciples were first called Christians at Antioch.' Acts 11:25, 26

The disciples who first brought the gospel to Antioch did not limit their concern to Jews, but 'began to speak to Greeks also'. This church thus became the first to contain a large Gentile element. It was fast-growing and energetic. It sent money for famine relief to the church in Jerusalem. At Antioch 'overseas missions' were born when the church sent out Barnabas and Paul. The church challenged those in Jerusalem who insisted on Jewish traditions. It had been a master-stroke by Barnabas to fetch his friend Saul back from Tarsus to help with the teaching of this lively and strategic community.

This city, on the River Orontes, was capital of the Roman province of Syria and third largest in the Empire. Today the town is called Antakya, in the south-east corner of Turkey.

Salamis today consists of extensive ruins scattered over an area of sand-dune and woodland near Famagusta. The theatre, gymnasium (pictured here), harbour and other remains evoke something of the prosperous city which confronted the missionaries on this first stop on their first journey.

Cyprus

'While they were worshipping the Lord and fasting, the Holy Spirit said, "Set apart for me Barnabas and Saul for the work to which I have called them." . . . *The two of them, sent on their way by the Holy Spirit, went down to Seleucia and sailed from there to Cyprus. When they arrived at Salamis, they proclaimed the word of God in the Jewish synagogues* . . . *They travelled through the whole island until they came to Paphos* . . .' Acts 13:2, 4-6

Paul and Barnabas visited first the island which was the birth-place both of Barnabas himself and of some of the very first evangelists to Antioch. They found a predominantly Roman culture, but also, as everywhere around the Mediterranean, Jewish synagogues. They set the pattern for their future work by preaching first in these synagogues.

Paphos, at the other end of Cyprus, was where Paul met the proconsul Sergius Paulus. The Roman ruins pictured here may have been the proconsul's residence; or remains of the forum.

Today extensive Roman, Hellenistic and Byzantine ruins surround the harbour from which Paul and Barnabas sailed for the next stage of their mission.

Pisidian Antioch

'From Paphos, Paul and his companions sailed to Perga in Pamphylia . . . From Perga they went on to Pisidian Antioch. On the Sabbath they entered the synagogue . . . Standing up, Paul motioned with his hand and said: "Men of Israel and you Gentiles who worship God, listen to me! . . ."'
Acts 13:13–16

In making first for Perga (see page 237) and then Antioch in Pisidia, Paul pursued the same policy which later took him to Athens and Rome. He deliberately made for main centres from which the gospel would be taken to the surrounding districts by the converts rather than the missionaries.

The record in the Acts of Paul's address in the synagogue at Pisidian Antioch is very full and detailed. It may give a summary of the way he used such opportunities. It is a forceful statement of Jewish history, showing that Jesus is the promised Messiah, followed by an account of what happened to Jesus and what his death and resurrection mean. Throughout, he interprets the gospel as a fulfilment of the Old Testament.

Pisidian Antioch was a centre of Hellenistic Greek and Roman culture with a considerable Jewish settlement. High in what is now central Turkey, it has a magnificent setting. The Roman aqueducts pictured here once brought water to the city, which now lies in ruins.

Lystra

'When the crowd saw what Paul had done, they shouted in the Lycaonian language, "The gods have come down to us in human form!" Barnabas they called Zeus, and Paul they called Hermes because he was the chief speaker. The priest of Zeus, whose temple was just outside the city, brought bulls and wreaths to the city gates because he and the crowd wanted to offer sacrifices to them . . .' Acts 14:11–13

At Lystra, Paul and Barnabas were faced, not now with Jews, but with naïve and superstitious pagans. The tactics they adopted show the flexibility of approach which made them such great missionaries. They made the starting-point of their teaching God the Creator, 'the living God, who made heaven and earth . . .'

The setting of Lystra is a landscape of rocks, mountains and fertile plain. Today the site of Lystra itself is no more than a litter of fallen stones.

Head of Hermes, found at Pergamum (Izmir Archaeological Museum).

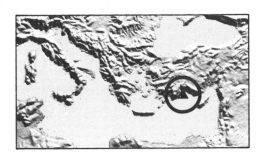

Attalia

'When they had preached the word in Perga, they went down to Attalia. From Attalia they sailed back to Antioch, where they had been committed to the grace of God for the work they had now completed.' Acts 14:25, 26

On the return journey to Antioch in Syria, Paul and Barnabas passed through all the towns in Asia Minor where they had preached before. Visiting the new churches, 'they committed them to the Lord in whom they had put their trust.'

A trading schooner lies in the small harbour of the modern resort town of Antalya, formerly Attalia, on the south coast of Turkey.

Extensive ruins remain at Perga, a short distance inland, which the missionaries visited on both their outward and return journeys.

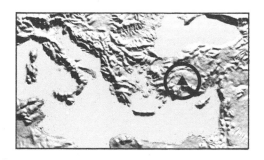

Pisidia

'Some time later Paul said to Barnabas, "Let us go back and visit the brothers in all the towns where we preached the word of the Lord and see how they are doing."' Acts 15:36

On their return from this first great journey Paul and Barnabas reported back to the church in Antioch which had sent them out, and then had to defend the young Gentile church at the council of Jerusalem. On the second missionary journey, they retraced their steps, before breaking new ground. Their route took them hundreds of miles across the mountains and plains of what is now central Turkey.

Neapolis

'During the night Paul had a vision of a man of Macedonia standing and begging him, "Come over to Macedonia and help us." After Paul had seen the vision, we got ready at once to leave for Macedonia, concluding that God had called us to preach the gospel to them. From Troas we put out to sea and sailed straight for Samothrace, and the next day on to Neapolis . . .'
Acts 16:9–11

Neapolis, modern Kavalla in northern Greece, was the port for Philippi. Samothrace is an island in the Aegean Sea, between Turkey and Greece.

As the missionaries stepped ashore at Neapolis, they brought the gospel for the first time to Europe. Luke's account changes suddenly at Troas from 'they' to 'we': he had now joined Paul and his companions himself. Was he the man from Macedonia whose urgent requests for help gave Paul his night time vision of the need 'to go on into Macedonia'?

Certainly Luke was a great asset to the Christian cause. Historical scholars have set Luke's Gospel and the Acts of the Apostles alongside other historical writing of antiquity. They find Luke compares highly favourably with most of them. The accuracy of his historical detail is exceptional and has revealed facts about the world of his time, which would not otherwise be known. He is probably unique among Bible writers in not being a Jew, with the result that his writing is sensitive to the background and understanding of a Gentile readership.

Luke's interest and experience in medicine shows through at several points in the story, where he uses precise medical terms to describe the sicknesses Jesus and the apostles healed.

Philippi

'. . . From there we travelled to Philippi, a Roman colony and the leading city of that district of Macedonia. And we stayed there several days. On the Sabbath we went outside the city gate to the river, where we expected to find a place of prayer . . .' Acts 16:12, 13

Paul again made straight for the leading city of the district. The result was a striking example of the effectiveness of this policy. Among the first converts was Lydia, a 'dealer in purple goods' who came from Thyatira, a leading city in Asia Minor. By the time the book of Revelation was written, there was a church established there.

It was at Philippi that Paul and his companion Silas were imprisoned. When a minor earth tremor opened the prison doors, they stayed where they were and kept order among the other prisoners. This so impressed the gaoler, who was certain there had been a mass escape and was on the point of suicide, that he 'believed in the Lord Jesus and was saved'.

The official names translated as 'authorities', 'magistrates', and 'officers' are precise and reflect Philippi's civic pride in its status as a Roman colony.

The picture is of the Forum at Philippi, with the ruins of a Byzantine basilica behind. Several places nearby could have been the 'riverside' where the women met to pray, though some of the streams have recently been drained in the interests of mosquito control and irrigation.

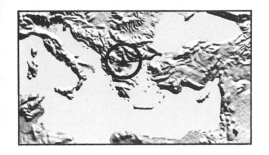

The road to Thessalonica

'When they had passed through Amphipolis and Apollonia, they came to Thessalonica, where there was a Jewish synagogue. As his custom was, Paul went into the synagogue, and on three Sabbath days he reasoned with them from the Scriptures, explaining and proving that the Christ had to suffer and rise from the dead. "This Jesus I am proclaiming to you is the Christ," he said.' Acts 17:1-3

Paul and Silas had extended debates with the Jews of Thessalonica, and some believed. But the majority eventually became so opposed to their preaching that they turned the mob against them and drove them from the town. The missionaries moved on to Berea, where things went better at first, but the anger of the Thessalonian Jews reached here too and life was made so intolerable that they had to leave.

The Via Egnatia was the main east-west Roman road, linking the west coast of Greece with what is now Istanbul. The stone slabs worn into ruts by the wheels of the traffic were those on which Paul and his companions trod as they made for Thessalonica, then as now the most prominent city of the region.

Today Thessaloniki is the second largest city in Greece. In later Roman times the Via Egnatia passed under the Arch of Galerius pictured here. The street is still called by the same name.

245

Athens

'While Paul was waiting for them in Athens, he was greatly distressed to see that the city was full of idols. So he reasoned in the synagogue with the Jews and the God-fearing Greeks, as well as in the market-place day by day with those who happened to be there . . . they took him and brought him to a meeting of the Areopagus, where they said to him, "May we know what this new teaching is you are presenting?"' Acts 17:16, 17, 19

Athens was the cultural heart of the ancient world, the centre of the 'hellenistic' culture and Greek common language which was the setting for so much of Paul's travels. The city was also the meeting-place of every different type of religious belief and practice. Paul was appalled. He took every opportunity to tell of the one true God who had raised Jesus from the dead.

As at pagan but rural Lystra, so now in sophisticated Athens, Paul started back at the beginning, with God as Creator. Here too he adapted his presentation of Christianity to the cultural understanding of the people. He quoted their poets, took up their doubts about idolatry, and took them on to a powerful declaration of Jesus as the risen Lord.

Behind the agora, or market-place, at Athens rises the Acropolis (to the left), and Mars Hill, or the Areopagus (to the right). It was this hill which gave its name to the Council of the Areopagus which formerly met there. In Paul's day it met in one of the colonnaded buildings flanking the agora itself. It was before this learned body that Paul was taken to submit his 'new teaching'.

The Acropolis of Athens was a fortified sanctuary which was both the centre of its worship and its ultimate defensive position against invaders. The Parthenon, with which it is crowned, was built in the fifth century BC, the 'golden age' of Athens under Pericles. It has been successively a temple to the goddess Athena, a church, a mosque, a gunpowder store – and a shrine of classicism and tourism.

247

Corinth

'Many of the Corinthians who heard Paul believed and were baptised. One night the Lord spoke to him in a vision: "Do not be afraid . . . I have many people in this city." So Paul stayed for a year and a half, teaching them the word of God. While Gallio was proconsul of Achaia, the Jews made a united attack on Paul and brought him into court . . .' Acts 18:8–12

Paul's stay in Corinth was long and fruitful. It seems his best results came when he gave up teaching in the synagogue and began operating from the house of a God-fearing Gentile next door. Those who responded seem to have included both Gentiles and Jews. The incident when he was accused before the Roman proconsul provides an indication of the fair-mindedness of the Roman authorities.

The temple of Apollo dominates the ancient site of Corinth today. Behind rises the fortress of Acro-Corinth. Near the temple the agora, or market-place, contains the remains of shops, temples, fountains, houses – and the 'bema', the official rostrum from which the Roman governor spoke. See too the picture on page 266.

Ephesus: the temple

'You see and hear how this fellow Paul has convinced and led astray large numbers of people here in Ephesus and in practically the whole province of Asia. He says that man-made gods are no gods at all. There is danger not only that our trade will lose its good name, but also that the temple of the great goddess Artemis will be discredited, and the goddess herself, who is worshipped throughout the province of Asia and the world, will be robbed of her divine majesty . . .' Acts 19:26, 27

Two aspects of religious life in Ephesus emerge from the Acts' account of Paul's time there: a preoccupation with occult practices, and a hard commercialism. As his gospel preaching began to have an effect, he met opposition from both.

He started as usual by teaching in the synagogue, but when Jewish hostility made that impossible he hired a local lecture-hall. This led to considerable interest in Christianity, and some local exorcists tried to use the name of Jesus in casting out demons. When this badly misfired, many people from both the Jewish and the Greek communities surrendered all the objects connected with their occult practices. (Typically, the value of this haul was precisely reckoned up.)

However, the commercial side of religion in Ephesus proved harder to overcome. When Demetrius and his fellow silversmiths found that the effects of the Christian gospel were threatening their trade in 'silver shrines of Artemis', they provoked a massive riot.

The great temple of Artemis, or Diana, was one of the wonders of the ancient world. The large rectangular area, which was until recently marsh and water littered with broken pillars, has now been cleared.

The nearby Museum of Ephesus contains two larger-than-life statues of the goddess. This one is a Roman version in white marble. Diana was the Roman goddess of chastity, Artemis the Greek goddess of love. It is typical of the place that the two were identified – and merged with the ancient local fertility cults.

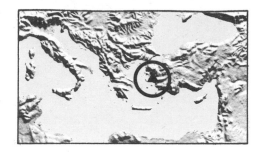

Ephesus: the theatre

'. . . When they heard this, they were furious and began shouting: "Great is Artemis of the Ephesians!" Soon the whole city was in an uproar. The people . . . rushed as one man into the theatre . . . The assembly was in confusion . . . The city clerk quietened the crowd and said: "Men of Ephesus, doesn't all the world know that the city of Ephesus is the guardian of the temple of the great Artemis and of her image, which fell from heaven? Therefore, since these facts are undeniable, you ought to be quiet and not do anything rash . . ."' Acts 19:28–29, 32, 35–36

The riot in the theatre must have been terrifying. It was a huge amphitheatre, and held a large number of people. Although the city clerk finally quietened the riot with great diplomatic skill, the atmosphere left in the city

The main street at Ephesus. Hadrian's temple (see page 270) is on the left.

The theatre is but one of the magnificent and extensive remains still being uncovered by archaeologists at Ephesus. The road leads down to what was once the harbour, long since silted up.

would have been dangerously abrasive. Paul felt the time had come to move on.

But the church he left behind was to prove strong and well-organized. It is first mentioned when the Jews there were visited by the Alexandrian Jew, Apollos. Sympathetic to Christianity, he had nevertheless only a partial grasp of the faith, being wholly ignorant of the Holy Spirit. And so, when Paul returned to the city a little later, he found a small group of people following Jesus, but who 'had not even heard of the Holy Spirit'. He put them straight on this vital belief, and their resulting experience of spiritual life made an ideal support to the teaching Paul gave over the next two years about the kingdom of God.

Miletus, 50 miles/80km by road from Ephesus, was another of the great cosmopolitan cities of the west coast of Asia Minor, colonies of Hellenistic Greek culture. Like Ephesus, it boasts the remains of a magnificent theatre. Seat reservations are inscribed on the stone seats, including one for Jews and God-fearers.

Miletus

'From Miletus, Paul sent to Ephesus for the elders of the church. When they arrived, he said to them: "You know how I lived the whole time I was with you, from the first day I came into the province of Asia. I served the Lord with great humility and with tears, although I was severely tested . . . And now, compelled by the Spirit, I am going to Jerusalem, not knowing what will happen to me there . . ."' Acts 20:17–19, 22

Paul's return from his third missionary journey was hurried. He wanted to reach Jerusalem as soon as he could. But since his ship had to put in at Miletus, he took the opportunity to ask the elders of the young church at Ephesus to meet him there.

His address to them is quite different from anything else in the Acts. Most of his other addresses persuaded people of the truth of Christianity. But this one is spoken to Christian pastors, to guide them in their life together and in the care of their flock.

Paul reminded the Ephesian elders at Miletus to look after their flock as shepherds protect their sheep from marauding wolves.

It is a very moving speech, in which he reminds them they will never meet again. Pointing to the example of his own life alongside them, he urges these church elders to love and serve the Christian community. He calls them to be 'shepherds of the church of God, which he bought with his own blood'.

This encounter reveals Paul as more than a persuasive missionary. He was a deeply caring pastor to the Christians in the cities he had visited.

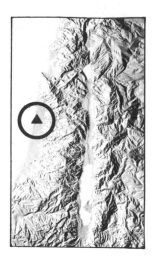

Roman pillars are washed by the sea in what remains of Caesarea; they were used to strengthen Crusader walls.

Statues, a theatre, a horse-racing stadium, aqueduct, and remains of harbour breakwaters are left from Roman times. An inscription bearing the name of Pontius Pilate was unearthed in 1961.

Caesarea

'So the soldiers, carrying out their orders, took Paul with them during the night and brought him as far as Antipatris. The next day they let the cavalry go on with him, while they returned to the barracks. When the cavalry arrived in Caesarea, they delivered the letter to the governor and handed Paul over to him.' Acts 23:31–33

Paul had already passed through Caesarea on his way to Jerusalem. When he returned it was under Roman guard. His visit to the Jerusalem temple nearly provoked a lynching, and even after the Roman troops took him into protective custody, his Jewish antagonists still plotted his assassination. So not surprisingly governor Felix found him a very interesting prisoner – all the more so because Paul was a Roman citizen and Caesarea the centre of local Roman government.

There followed three very different trials, in each of which Paul made a vigorous and effective defence. Felix found Paul pricking his conscience a bit too sharply for comfort, and temporized for two long years. His successor, Festus, understood far less about Jewish matters, so Paul appealed to Caesar. But before he could be sent to the hub of the Empire, King Herod Agrippa arrived in Caesarea and asked to hear him. Felix and Festus were both Romans, but Agrippa was a Jew, grandson of Herod the Great. Before him, Paul told once again the dramatic story of his conversion on the Damascus road.

'This man could have been set free,' said Agrippa to Festus, 'if he had not appealed to Caesar.' But at least part of Paul's purpose in appealing was to create the occasion to declare the gospel in Rome itself.

Malta

'When daylight came, they did not recognise the land, but they saw a bay with a sandy beach, where they decided to run the ship aground if they could . . . But the ship struck a sand-bar and ran aground. The bow stuck fast and would not move, and the stern was broken to pieces by the pounding of the surf. Once safely on shore, we found out that the island was called Malta.'
Acts 27:39, 41; 28:1

On the journey to Rome, delays meant a departure from Crete dangerously late in the year. Paul advised against it, but was overruled. The ship was caught by a gale, driven westwards across the Mediterranean by the late-season 'Euraquilo' winds. Luke graphically describes the increasingly desperate efforts made to save the ship. But eventually the ship stuck: luckily enough in a reasonably hospitable bay on the coast of Malta. The ship was lost. But passengers and crew managed to scramble to safety.

The shipwreck meant a three-month delay in the journey. But the travellers' misfortune was the island's gain: many, including the governor's father, found healing through Paul's prayers.

St Paul's Bay, as it is called today, is 8½ miles/13km along the coast of Malta from modern Valetta. It meets precisely the conditions of the description in Acts. A shallow sand-bank runs out from the distant spit of land: it was this the ship struck while they were making for the beach beyond.

The road to Rome

'And so we went to Rome. The brothers there had heard that we were coming, and they travelled as far as the Forum of Appius and the Three Taverns to meet us. At the sight of these men Paul thanked God and was encouraged.' Acts 28:14, 15

So Paul arrived in Rome, capital of the Empire. We can only guess how the Christians who came out to meet him came to be there. No doubt believers moved there in the ordinary course of business and brought the gospel with them. The dominance of Rome had made national borders insignificant and had opened up communications right round the Mediterranean world. It was a highly mobile society, and this made conditions ideal for the rapid spread of the good news about Christ.

Outside Rome the ancient Roman road, the Via Appia, is lined with monuments. Stretches of original paving, rutted by cartwheels, are still used by modern traffic.

Rome

'For two whole years Paul stayed there in his own rented house and welcomed all who came to see him. Boldly and without hindrance he preached the kingdom of God and taught about the Lord Jesus Christ.' Acts 28:30, 31

Paul had reached the heart of the ancient world. His imprisonment was relatively open, though he would always have had a soldier chained to him. At least this provided an ideal opportunity both to teach the Christians and to preach to the city's Jews and Gentiles. Whether Paul was able to realize his ambition to take the gospel to Spain, or whether he lived in Rome until his death, we do not know. The book of Acts comes to rather an abrupt end . . . but the work of the gospel went on.

The Colosseum, the enormous amphitheatre built in AD 80, took its name from the colossal statue of Nero that stood near it. Here 45,000 spectators could watch fights between gladiators, even simulated naval battles. Here, when persecution later reached its height, Christians were thrown to lions to make sport for the crowds.

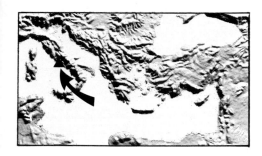

The Forum at Rome was the city centre with its main public buildings. It was the city's principal meeting-place.

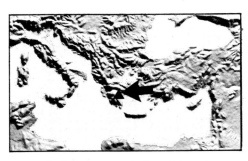

Corinth was an industrial and trading city with a proverbial reputation for immorality. Cargoes shipped between Rome and the Aegean were unloaded at Corinth, hauled by road across the narrow isthmus, and loaded on to another ship to continue their journey. This avoided the hazardous voyage round the southern tip of the Peloponnese. The Lechaion road in this picture led to the principal port. (See also page 248).

8
LETTERS TO THE CHURCHES

Romans

'Greet Priscilla and Aquila, my fellow-workers in Christ Jesus . . . Greet also the church that meets at their house. Greet my dear friend Epenetus . . .' Romans 16:3–5

Paul's letter to the Romans is his chief statement of what the gospel is. He describes the dilemma of a world which knew God but had turned against him. All have sinned, Gentile and Jew alike. And God is holy: he cannot simply overlook sin. But God sent his Son to die, to take the death penalty upon himself. With faith in Jesus Christ alone, we can be justified: declared just before God. But the lesson is not only about belief; there is also plenty of practical application, and it closes with a list of personal greetings. Paul wrote to people he knew and loved.

Corinthians

'The body is a unit, though it is made up of many parts; and though all its parts are many, they form one body. So it is with Christ. For we were all baptised by one Spirit into one body – whether Jews or Greeks, slave or free . . .'
1 Corinthians 12:12, 13

▷

Paul wrote two letters to the church in Corinth, in AD 54 and 56. In the first he tries to put right their failings in unity, in sexual morality, idolatry, worship and belief in the resurrection. Many of the problems this letter reveals arose from the particular situation of the city. The party divisions reflected the mixed population; there was open immorality; meat sold in the market came from pagan sacrifices; women must be veiled to avoid suspicion of prostitution; there were extremes of emphasis on Greek philosophy, or on ecstatic spiritual gifts associated with the mystery religions.

The second letter has to counter a different problem. Paul has to answer attacks on his authority as an apostle. In his defence he gives a deeply-felt account of the true concerns and pressures of Christian ministry.

An unusually large Jewish synagogue, dating from the early centuries AD, has been found at Sardis (one of the 'seven churches' of Revelation). The church in Galatia had been troubled by some who advocated keeping the whole Jewish law.

Galatians

'You foolish Galatians! Who has bewitched you? Before your very eyes Jesus Christ was clearly portrayed as crucified. I would like to learn just one thing from you: Did you receive the Spirit by observing the law, or by believing what you heard?' Galatians 3:1, 2

It is a matter of debate whether Paul wrote to churches in the whole Roman province of Galatia (including Pontus, Phrygia, Pisidia etc.), or simply those among the 'Galatian' or 'Gallic' people. They were an ethnic group who had settled in the northern part of the Roman province after coming from central Europe in the third century BC. But the purpose of the letter is clear: to prevent the churches giving in to Jewish elements who were denying the gospel by preaching 'salvation by law-keeping'. It was vital that Christianity should become more than just a branch of Judaism. People are saved by faith in Christ, not by keeping the law. The Christian life is described as freedom in the Spirit.

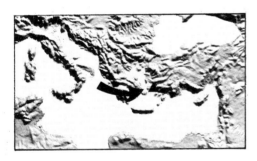

One of the temples at Ephesus was dedicated to Hadrian, the Roman Emperor some sixty years after Paul wrote to the Ephesians. It shows something of the splendour of the buildings of the time (see too page 252), and also graphically illustrates the Emperor-worship which was to become a cause of persecution of the Christians, for whom Jesus alone is Lord.

Ephesians

'You are no longer foreigners and aliens, but fellow-citizens with God's people and members of God's household, built on the foundation of the apostles and prophets, with Christ Jesus himself as the chief corner-stone. In him the whole building is joined together and rises to become a holy temple in the Lord. And in him you too are being built together to become a dwelling in which God lives by his Spirit.' Ephesians 2:19–22

Paul begins this letter by showing that God has a great, eternal plan, which has been brought to fruition in the life, death and resurrection of Christ. God's purpose is not just to save individuals, but to bring them together as a new community, the church. He uses two picture-words for this community: the 'body of Christ', with all its different parts functioning in harmony, and the 'bride of Christ', whom he loves. Paul prays that the Christians at Ephesus will learn 'how wide and long and high and deep is the love of Christ'. Towards the end of the letter he urges them to 'put on the whole armour of God', so as to be equipped for a world of spiritual conflict.

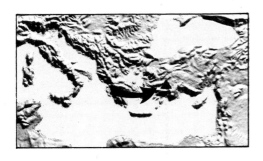

Colossae was across a broad fertile valley from Laodicea and Hierapolis (see page 281). The mound of the ancient town, lying near the village of Honaz in the background of the picture, is yet to be excavated.

Colossians

'Christ is the image of the invisible God, the firstborn over all creation. For by him all things were created . . . For God was pleased to have all his fulness dwell in him, and through him to reconcile to himself all things . . .'
Colossians 1:15, 16, 19, 20

Paul had never visited Colossae. The church there was founded through the work of his colleague Epaphras, operating from Ephesus. But he writes to them full of concern to draw them back to true Christianity from the teachings of 'gnosticism'.

This half-pagan system of belief combined nature mysticism with speculations on created and uncreated beings. It would have appealed to a predominantly agricultural community in an area surrounded by mountains. As long ago as Heraclitus in the sixth century BC the people had been convinced that 'the world is full of spiritual beings'. Paul wrote that Christ is the supreme Lord of all creation. He alone can reconcile people to God.

The letters of Peter

'You have been born again, not of perishable seed, but of imperishable, through the living and enduring word of God. For, "All men are like grass, and all their glory is like the flowers of the field . . ."' 1 Peter 1:23, 24

Peter wrote to Christians in churches spread round what is now Turkey. His aim was to strengthen them in face of coming persecution and trials. In doing so he used vivid images they would appreciate: seedtime and harvest, flocks and shepherds, 'waterless springs and mists driven by a storm'. He encouraged them by showing that suffering can have a positive value, refining faith as fire refines gold. Repeatedly he brought them back to the changeless essentials: eternal life, the gospel message itself – truths which not even death can take away.

Smyrna

'Write on a scroll what you see and send it to the seven churches: to Ephesus, Smyrna, Pergamum, Thyatira, Sardis, Philadelphia and Laodicea . . . Do not be afraid of what you are about to suffer. I tell you, the devil will put some of you in prison to test you . . . Be faithful, even to the point of death, and I will give you the crown of life.'
Revelation 1:11; 2:10

The apostle John was exiled in his old age on the island of Patmos, off the coast of Turkey. There he had a vision of Christ in heaven, who told him to record the many images which were then revealed to him. The result is a dramatic and highly-coloured piece of 'apocalyptic' writing – a literary form of the time which used vivid symbolism to communicate a message. He may have used this style partly to disguise its anti-Roman thrust; or simply because it was the only way he could convey in universal terms his picture of the lordship of Christ in history.

The first part of the book of Revelation is a series of letters to seven churches on the mainland, in the order in which a messenger would reach them.

A later leader of the church at Smyrna was Bishop Polycarp. Before his martyrdom in AD 155, he was to say of his master Jesus: 'Eighty-six years have I served him, and he has done me no wrong; how then can I blaspheme my king who saved me?'

Smyrna, the second of the towns the messenger would have reached with John's letter, is today the busy industrial seaport city of Izmir. The Forum, pictured here, is the chief evidence of a Roman past in which the town was famous for its magnificent public buildings.

Away from the main acropolis of Pergamum is the ruin of a temple of Asclepius, the god of healing. Under the floor were water conduits; behind the arch is the end of a tunnel which may have been used for some sort of shock therapy for nervous disease. Medical treatment was mixed with mystery religion: its pagan immorality may underlie some of the references in John's letter.

Pergamum

'I know where you live – where Satan has his throne. Yet you remain true to my name.'
Revelation 2:13

One of the seven letters in Revelation is addressed to the church in Pergamum. Christ commends them for holding firm. But in the crucible of persecution certain impurities have appeared. He urges the Christians in each of the churches to resist the temptations of false teaching and of compromise.

Temple dedicated to the Emperor Trajan.

On a great rocky acropolis overlooking the small Turkish town of Bergama are the remains of the ancient town of Pergamum. Behind the theatre is the site of the great altar of Zeus. Pergamum was not only a centre for the worship of the traditional gods, Zeus, Dionysus and Athena, but the place where the worship of the Roman Emperor first took hold.

A few miles from Laodicea are the hot springs of Hierapolis. The two towns were mentioned together by Paul in his letter to Colossae, also nearby. The water was channelled along conduits to Laodicea itself – and would have arrived tepid.

Laodicea

'I know your deeds, that you are neither cold nor hot. I wish you were either one or the other! So, because you are lukewarm – neither hot nor cold – I am about to spit you out of my mouth . . .'
Revelation 3:15, 16

Christ condemned the church in Laodicea not only for its lukewarm devotion, but also for reckoning itself richer in faith than it really was. This complacency came from living in a wealthy commercial and banking centre. Christ had to tell them they were in total poverty unless they became rich in their wholehearted commitment to him.

Mineral deposits from the water formed on the conduits, and have made them solid and permanent.

The waters from Hierapolis flow over cliffs. Over the centuries the mineral deposits have built up into terraces and lime 'waterfalls'.

From the site of Laodicea itself the white cliffs of Hierapolis can be seen in the distance. Laodicea was also a commercial centre for banking and the wool trade, and a medical centre: gold, clothing and eye-salve are all alluded to in John's letter.

Judgement and glory

'Woe! Woe, O great city . . . In one hour she has been brought to ruin! Rejoice over her, O heaven! Rejoice, saints and apostles and prophets! God has judged her for the way she treated you . . . Then I heard what sounded like a great multitude . . . shouting: "Hallelujah! For our Lord God Almighty reigns. Let us rejoice and be glad and give him glory!"' Revelation 18:19, 20; 19:6, 7

Revelation was written against the background of persecution and martyrdom, probably in the reign of Emperor Domitian (81–96). It was written to encourage endurance to the end. To do this, John turned the eyes of his readers to realities beyond the unpleasant reality that faced them in their day. He looked to a time in the future when the persecuting Roman Empire ('Babylon' in his Old Testament imagery) would be overthrown. And he looked to an eternal, spiritual dimension: 'now have come the salvation and the power and the kingdom of our God, and the authority of his Christ'.

The final vision is of 'the new Jerusalem', when the rule of God will be fully established and his people removed from everything that hurts and spoils their lives. The constant theme is of worship of God for his victory in Christ.

Poppies among the ruins of Philippi are testimony to the passing of the pagan civilization of New Testament times.

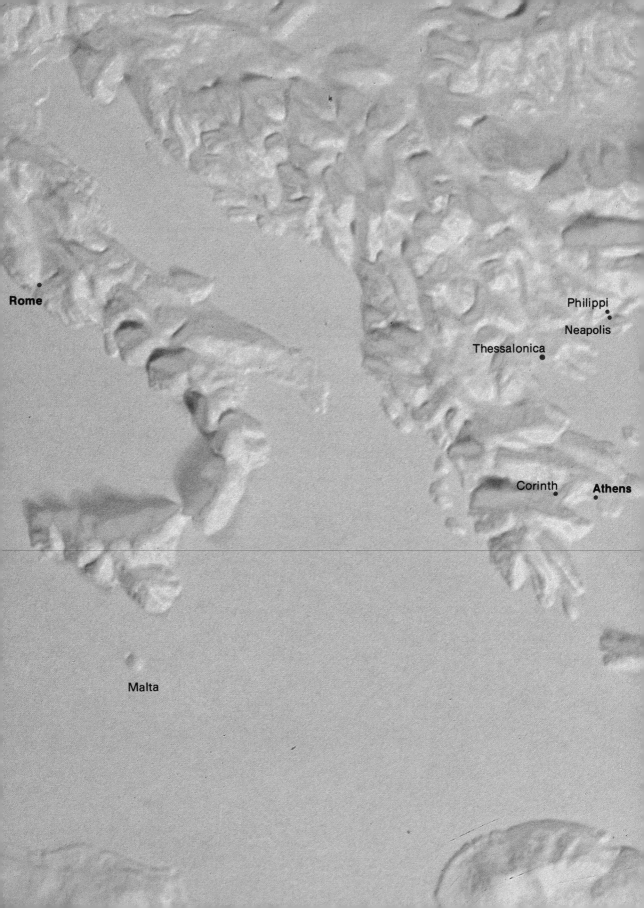

Rome

Philippi

Neapolis

Thessalonica

Corinth   **Athens**

Malta

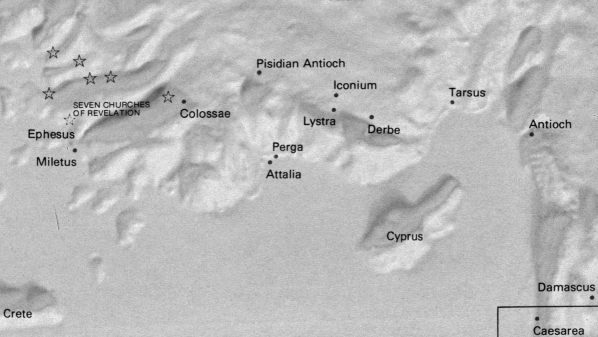

Galatia

Pisidian Antioch

Iconium

Tarsus

★
★
★
★
SEVEN CHURCHES
OF REVELATION
★
★

Colossae

Lystra

Derbe

Antioch

Ephesus

Perga

Miletus

Attalia

Cyprus

Crete

Damascus

Caesarea

Joppa

Jerusalem

See
page 144